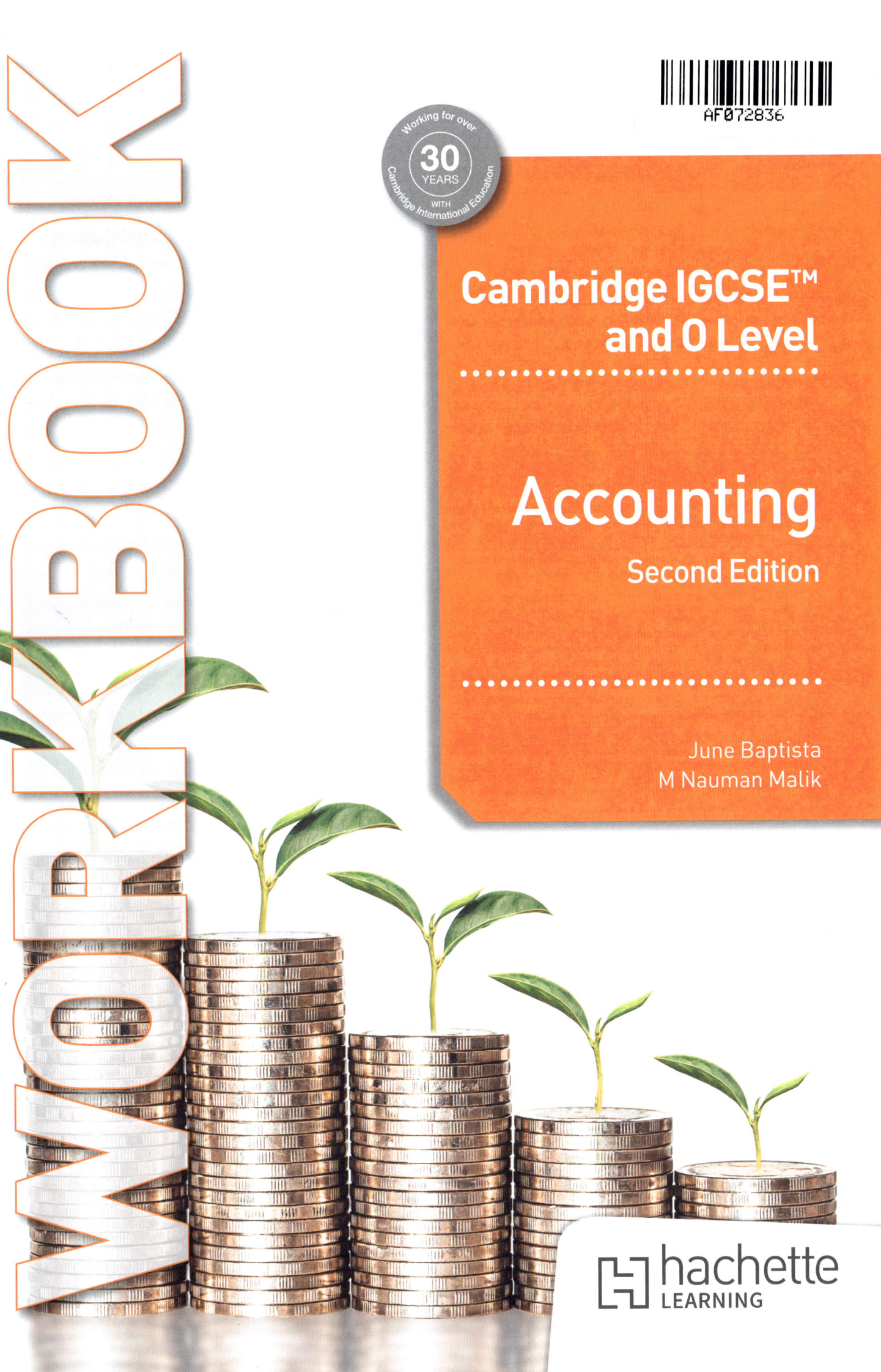

Introduction

Welcome to the Cambridge IGCSE™ and O Level Accounting Workbook. The aim of this workbook is to provide you with further opportunity to practise the skills you have acquired through using the Cambridge IGCSE and O Level Accounting Student's Book. It is designed to complement the Student's Book and to provide additional exercises to support you throughout the course and help you to prepare for examinations.

The chapters in this workbook reflect the topics in the Student's Book. There is no set way to approach using this Workbook. You may wish to use it to supplement your understanding of the different topics as you work through each chapter of the Student's Book, or you may prefer to use it to reinforce your skills in dealing with particular topics as you prepare for examination. It is intended to be sufficiently flexible to suit whatever you feel is the best approach for your needs. Answer lines have been provided but do not necessarily indicate length of response. You may need additional paper for some questions. You may also need to copy some of the financial documents that you are asked to complete.

This text has not been through the endorsement process for the Cambridge Pathway.
Any references or materials related to answers, grades, papers or examinations are based on the opinion of the author(s).

The Cambridge International Education syllabus or curriculum framework associated assessment guidance material and specimen papers should always be referred to for definitive guidance.

The questions and sample answers that appear in this book were written by the authors.
In examinations, the way marks are awarded may be different.

Although every effort has been made to ensure that website addresses are correct at time of going to press, Hachette Learning cannot be held responsible for the content of any website mentioned in this book. It is sometimes possible to find a relocated web page by typing in the address of the home page for a website in the URL window of your browser.

Hachette UK's policy is to use papers that are natural, renewable and recyclable products and made from wood grown in well-managed forests and other controlled sources. The logging and manufacturing processes are expected to conform to the environmental regulations of the country of origin.

To order, please visit www.hachettelearning.com or contact Customer Service
at education@hachette.co.uk / +44 (0)1235 827827.

ISBN: 9781036010638

© M Nauman Malik and June Baptista 2025

First published in 2018
This second edition published 2025 by Hachette Learning,
An Hachette UK Company
Carmelite House, 50 Victoria Embankment, London EC4Y 0DZ
www.hachettelearning.com

The authorised representative in the EEA is Hachette Ireland, 8 Castlecourt Centre, Dublin 15, D15 XTP3, Ireland (email: info@hbgi.ie)

Impression number   10 9 8 7 6 5 4 3 2 1

Year   2028 2027 2026 2025

All rights reserved. Apart from any use permitted under UK copyright law, no part of this publication may be reproduced or transmitted in any form or by any means, electronic or mechanical, including photocopying and recording, or held within any information storage and retrieval system, without permission in writing from the publisher or under licence from the Copyright Licensing Agency Limited. Further details of such licences (for reprographic reproduction) may be obtained from the Copyright Licensing Agency Limited, www.cla.co.uk.

Cover photo © thanmano - stock.adobe.com
Typeset in OfficianaSansStd-book 11.5/13 by Aptara Inc.
Printed in the UK by Bell & Bain Limited

A catalogue record for this title is available from the British Library

Contents

SECTION 1 The fundamentals of accounting
1. The purpose of accounting — 4
2. The accounting equation — 6

SECTION 2 Sources and recording of data
3. The double entry system of book-keeping — 9
4. Business documents — 14
5. Books of prime entry — 16

SECTION 3 Verification of accounting records
6. The trial balance — 24
7. Correction of errors — 26
8. Bank reconciliation — 29
9. Control accounts — 32

SECTION 4 Accounting procedures
10. Capital and revenue expenditure and receipts — 37
11. Accounting for depreciation and disposal of non-current assets — 39
12. Other payables and other receivables — 43
13. Irrecoverable debts and allowance for irrecoverable debts — 47
14. Valuation of inventory — 51

SECTION 5 Preparation of financial statements
15. Sole traders — 53
16. Partnerships — 58
17. Limited companies — 63
18. Clubs and societies — 67
19. Manufacturing accounts — 72
20. Incomplete records — 75

SECTION 6 Analysis and interpretation
21. Calculation and understanding of accounting ratios — 82
22. Interpretation of accounting ratios and inter-business comparisons — 85
23. Interested parties — 90
24. Limitations of accounting statements — 92

SECTION 7 Accounting concepts and modern practices
25. Accounting concepts — 94
26. Ethical considerations — 96
27. Technology and sustainability — 98

1 The fundamentals of accounting

Student's Book Chapters 1–2

1 The purpose of accounting

1 What is the purpose of double entry book-keeping?
   A To avoid errors
   B To calculate the owner's equity
   C To ensure no transaction is missing from the books
   D To record two entries for every transaction *[1 mark]*

2 How does an owner of a business make use of the business's financial statements?
   A To calculate the amount owing by trade receivables
   B To calculate the amount owing to trade payables
   C To check the bank statement balance
   D To monitor the progress being made by the business *[1 mark]*

3 Which statement about book-keeping and accounting is correct?
   A A book-keeper interprets financial statements
   B A book-keeper prepares financial statements
   C Accounting is dependent on the records maintained by a book-keeper
   D Accounting is only performed once every two years *[1 mark]*

4 What will financial data **not** include?
   A The excellent location for a clothing shop in a busy city
   B Purchases for the month of May
   C Return of damaged goods at cost
   D Value of a building owned by a business *[1 mark]*

5 Businesses make use of both book-keeping and accounting procedures. Explain why businesses use book-keeping. *[2 marks]*

....

....

....

6 Identify three reasons why a trader measures the business profit or loss. *[3 marks]*

....

....

....

....

1 The purpose of accounting

7 State five parties who might be interested in the financial statements of a business. *[5 marks]*

....

....

....

8 Complete the following table by writing the word 'true' or 'false' against each statement. *[5 marks]*

	True/False
A book-keeper needs more accounting skills than an accountant	
Book-keeping is carried out throughout the financial year	
Owners use financial statements to know the net worth of the business	
One of the main aims of a business is to make a profit	
Analysing financial statements is one of the tasks a manager does	

9 Explain the difference between:

  a accounting and book-keeping *[2 marks]*

....

....

....

....

  b financial and non-financial data *[2 marks]*

....

....

....

....

  c analysing and interpreting financial data *[2 marks]*

....

....

....

....

1 THE FUNDAMENTALS OF ACCOUNTING

10 State one reason why each of the following parties would be interested in a business' financial statements:

   a Banks [1 mark]

....

....

   b Investors and lenders [1 mark]

....

....

   c Suppliers [1 mark]

....

....

11 State one reason why a sole trader prepares financial statements. [1 mark]

....

....

2 The accounting equation

1 Why is a statement of financial position prepared by a sole trader?

   A To calculate the loss for the year

   B To calculate the owner's equity for the year

   C To record the transactions that took place during the financial year

   D To summarise what the business owns and what it owes [1 mark]

2 Which of these is a liability of a business?

   A Debts owing by credit customers

   B Debts owing by credit suppliers

   C Debts owing to credit suppliers

   D Loan given to a family member [1 mark]

3 What increases owner's equity?

   A Business expenses paid by the owner from their personal bank account

   B Business inventory taken by the owner for personal use

   C Cash taken out of the business for owner's personal use

   D Rent for owner's house paid using business cash [1 mark]

4 Which statement is **not** true?

   A Machinery is a current asset

   B Resources supplied to the business = resources owned by the business

   C The accounting equation is reflected in the statement of financial position

   D When an owner takes inventory for their own use, it is called drawings [1 mark]

5 Which of these is a business liability?

   A Bank loan

   B Cash

   C Machinery

   D Property [1 mark]

6 State the accounting equation. [1 mark]

....

2 The accounting equation

7 Define the following:

   a An asset [1 mark]

   ....

   b A liability [1 mark]

   ....

   c Owner's equity [1 mark]

   ....

   d The statement of financial position [1 mark]

   ....

   e A trade payable [1 mark]

   ....

8 Sylvester, a sole trader, had the following assets and liabilities on 31 December 2025:

	$
Equipment	50 000
Motor vehicle	10 000
Balance at bank	2 500
Debts owing to suppliers	3 800

Calculate Sylvester's owner's equity on 31 December 2025. Show your workings. [2 marks]

....

....

....

....

9 Complete the following table by placing a tick (✓) in the correct column to indicate whether each item is an asset or a liability. [10 marks]

	Asset	Liability
Motor van		
Trade receivables		
Long-term loan		
Property		
Bank overdraft		
Equipment		
Inventory		
Trade payables		
Cash in hand		

1 THE FUNDAMENTALS OF ACCOUNTING

10 Complete the following table to calculate the value of the missing items. *[6 marks]*

	Assets $	Liabilities $	Owner's equity $
a	4 500		1 800
b		35 700	49 500
c	7 890	6 350	
d	5 680		2 470
e		5 240	6 570
f	23 760	13 770	

11 Complete the following table with the words 'decrease' or 'increase' to show each transaction's effect on a business' assets, liabilities and owner's equity. The first one has been completed as an example. *[9 marks]*

	Transaction	Effect	
a	Bought goods on credit	Increase (inventory)	Increase (trade payables)
b	The owner introduced cash into business bank account		
c	The owner took money out of the business bank account for personal use		
d	The business sold goods for cash		
e	The business paid the amount owed to a trade payable by cheque		
f	The business sold goods on credit		
g	The business took a loan in cash		
h	A credit customer paid the business in cash		
i	The business bought a motor vehicle, paying by bank transfer		
j	The business paid back the loan by bank transfer		

12 Complete the following table with the words 'decrease' or 'increase' to show the effects of each transaction on assets, liabilities and owner's equity. The first one has been completed as an example. *[8 marks]*

	Assets	Liabilities	Owner's equity
Owner invested cash into the business	Increases		Increases
Machine bought by cheque			
Inventory bought on credit			
Inventory (goods) withdrawn by the owner for personal use			
Cash borrowed from a bank			
Furniture bought and payment made by owner's personal account			
Inventory bought on credit			

2 Sources and recording of data

Student's Book Chapters 3–5

3 The double entry system of book-keeping

1 Explain what is meant by the double entry system of book-keeping. *[2 marks]*

....

....

....

2 A sole trader buys inventory for cash. Which entries are made to record the transaction? *[1 mark]*

	Account debited	Account credited
A	Cash	Purchases
B	Purchases	Cash
C	Purchases	Trade payables
D	Trade payables	Purchases

3 A sole trader maintains their books using the double entry system. Which of the following is correct?

		Account debited	Account credited
a	Bought office furniture for cash	Cash	Purchases
b	A credit customer, K. Lala, pays by bank transfer	Bank	K. Lala
c	The owner introduced capital in cash	Cash	Capital
d	The owner withdrew cash for personal use	Capital	Cash

A a and b   **B** b and c   **C** c and d   **D** d and a   *[1 mark]*

4 Which statement is correct?

A Credit customers' accounts are not recorded in the books.

B Credit customers' accounts are recorded in the general ledger.

C Credit customers' accounts are recorded in the purchases ledger.

D Credit customers' accounts are recorded in the sales ledger. *[1 mark]*

5 Santiago returned damaged goods to his supplier, Nelson. How does Nelson record this in his books? *[1 mark]*

	Account debited	Account credited
A	Purchases returns	Santiago
B	Sales returns	Santiago
C	Santiago	Purchases returns
D	Santiago	Sales returns

6 Which closing balance will be listed as an asset in the statement of financial position?

A A credit balance on a supplier's account

B A credit balance on the bank account

C A debit balance on the drawings account

D A debit balance on the motor vehicle account *[1 mark]*

2 SOURCES AND RECORDING OF DATA

7 Sung Jin is a trader. The following account appeared in his ledger.

Monica Lee's account

Date 2024	Details	$	Date 2024	Details	$
Mar 6	Returns	35	Mar 1	Balance b/d	650
Mar 11	Bank	389	Mar 4	Purchases	340
	Discount	11			

a Identify the ledger in which Monica Lee's account would be kept in Sung Jin's books. *[1 mark]*

....

b i) Explain what the entry on 4 March records. *[1 mark]*

....

ii) Identify the account which would be debited in Sung Jin's books. *[1 mark]*

....

c Identify the ledger in which Sung Jin's account would be recorded in Monica Lee's books. *[1 mark]*

....

8 Bessy is a trader who maintains a complete set of accounting records.

a State **two** reasons why Bessy maintains accounts in different ledgers. *[2 marks]*

....

....

b Complete the following table to identify the ledger in which each account is found. *[7 marks]*

Account	Ledger
Motor vehicle	
Nadhim, a credit customer	
Purchases	
Sales	
Returns outwards	
Barry, a credit supplier	
Salaries	

9 State the difference between:

a an asset and a liability *[2 marks]*

....

....

....

b a non-current asset and a current asset [2 marks]

....

....

....

c a non-current liability and a current liability [2 marks]

....

....

....

d accounts that appear in a sales ledger and accounts that appear in a general ledger [2 marks]

....

....

....

e trade payables and trade receivables [2 marks]

....

....

....

10 a Explain the difference between the traditional 'T' Account format and the three-column running balance format for ledger accounts. [4 marks]

....

....

....

....

b Which of the methods referred to in part a) is typically used in manual accounting and why? [2 marks]

....

....

2 SOURCES AND RECORDING OF DATA

11 Ji Lui's statement of financial position was prepared on 31 December 2024. It showed the following assets and liabilities:

	$
Machinery	7 200
Trade receivables	800
Inventory	1 300
Other payables	830
Trade payables	510
Cash	180
Bank (debit balance)	250

a Calculate Ji Lui's owner's equity on 31 December 2024. *[2 marks]*

Assets = 7 200 + 800 + 1 300 + 180 + 250 = 9 730
Liabilities = 830 + 510 = 1 340
Owner's equity = 9 730 − 1 340 = $8 390

On 1 January 2025, the following transactions took place:

i) Ji Lui paid salaries for December 2024 in cash, $319.

ii) Ji Lui took cash of $89 for her personal use.

iii) Ji Lui transferred her private motor vehicle, $1 970, to the business.

iv) Ji Lui paid Ken Lee, a credit supplier, $98 by bank transfer, having received a cash discount of 2 per cent.

b State the double entry needed to record each transaction. *[5 marks]*

	Account(s) debited	$	Account(s) credited	$
i)	Other payables (Salaries)	319	Cash	319
ii)	Drawings	89	Cash	89
iii)	Motor vehicle	1 970	Capital	1 970
iv)	Ken Lee (Trade payables)	100	Bank	98
			Discount received	2

12 Simran's financial year end is 31 December. Her bank statements showed that her business had incurred the following bank charges.

2024	$
Mar 31	48
Jun 30	86
Sep 30	71
Dec 31	56

a Prepare the bank charges account in Simran's ledger for the year ended 31 December 2024, making the transfer to the statement of profit or loss. You can copy the ledger below. *[4 marks]*

Bank charges account						
Date	Details	$	Date	Details	$

b Explain why the total of bank charges is transferred to the statement of profit or loss instead of being carried down to the following year. *[4 marks]*

....

....

....

....

13 Pedro is a trader. The balance on his motor vehicles account at 1 January 2024 was $17 000.

On 31 October 2024, he bought a new vehicle costing $21 000 from Tip Top Motors. He paid $12 000 on that date by cheque, the balance being paid with a cheque for $1 000 each month, starting on 30 November 2024.

a Prepare the following ledger accounts for the year ended 31 December 2024. Bring down the balances on 1 January 2025. You can copy the ledgers below. *[10 marks]*

Motor vehicles account						
Date	Details	$	Date	Details	$

Tip Top Motors account						
Date	Details	$	Date	Details	$

2 SOURCES AND RECORDING OF DATA

b Explain why the balances on the accounts in a) were brought down and not transferred to the statement of profit or loss. *[4 marks]*

....

....

....

....

c Prepare the following ledger accounts for the year ended 31 December 2024 using a three-column running balance format. You can copy the ledgers below. *[7 marks]*

Motor vehicles account

Date	Details	Debit $	Credit $	Balance $

Tip Top Motors account

Date	Details	Debit $	Credit $	Balance $

4 Business documents

1 Lester, a sole trader, received the following business documents from his supplier, Wesley.

Date	Document	$
Jul 4	Invoice	540
Jul 11	Invoice	310
Jul 18	Credit note	110
Jul 25	Invoice	500
Aug 3	Invoice	260

No payments were made to Wesley during July, and his account had no opening balance.

What was the balance on 31 July on the statement of account sent by Wesley?

A $1 240

B $1 460

C $1 640

D $5 000 *[1 mark]*

2 Yusuf buys goods on credit from Jana, who issues an invoice. The goods are damaged, and Yusuf returns them to Jana without paying for them.

Which document should Jana issue to Yusuf on receipt of the returned goods?

A Credit note

B Debit note

C Purchases invoice

D Sales invoice *[1 mark]*

3 Why is a credit note sent?

A To allow for a trade discount

B To decrease the amount to be paid on an invoice

C To increase the amount due on an invoice

D To request payment in advance *[1 mark]*

4 Business documents

4 Which source documents would a business use to pay for purchases?

A Cheque

B Credit note

C Receipt

D Statement of account *[1 mark]*

5 Ahmed supplies goods to Jason on credit. A debit note is sent. Which statement is correct?

A Jason sends the debit note to Ahmed because he received damaged goods.

B Jason sends the debit note to Ahmed to order more goods.

C Ahmed uses the debit note to ask Jason to pay for goods he purchased on credit.

D Ahmed sends a debit note to Jason because only part of the order can be supplied. *[1 mark]*

6 Which detail is **not** typically included on a cheque counterfoil?

A Amount of the cheque

B Bank branch address

C Date of issue

D Payee's name *[1 mark]*

7 Which of these features is included in both manual and digital paying-in slips?

A Depositor's signature or digital authorisation

B Detailed listing of deposited items

C Electronic storage

D Both made of paper *[1 mark]*

8 Delphine ordered 500 boxes of nails from Ramesh. The price of each box was $15.10. Ramesh allowed a trade discount of 2 per cent. Calculate the total invoice Delphine received.

Show your workings. *[3 marks]*

....

....

....

9 a Complete the missing items (i) to (v) (words or figures) on the following document. *[5 marks]*

To: **K. Lui** 16 Charmaine's Place New Lynn		15 April 2025 From: **L. Kerry** Torbay	
Debit Note: 9			
Item	Quantity	Price per unit ($)	Total ($)
Fabric	3 bolts	20.25	(i)
Packets of bias binding	(ii)	5.00	100.00
			160.75
Less	(iii)	discount @ 1%	(iv)
			(v)

b Identify the sender of the note. *[1 mark]*

....

c Give one reason why the note is being sent. *[1 mark]*

....

2 SOURCES AND RECORDING OF DATA

10 Compare digital versions of cheque counterfoils and paying-in slips with their manual counterparts. *[4 marks]*

....

....

....

5 Books of prime entry

1 Which of these is both a book of prime entry and a ledger account?
   - **A** Cash book
   - **B** General journal
   - **C** Sales journal
   - **D** Sales return journal *[1 mark]*

2 Mi Kim, a sole trader, posts the total of her sales journal to the ledger at the end of each month. On 31 July 2024, the sales invoices net of trade discount for July were $4 000. Trade discounts amounted to $500.

   Which entry should be made in Mi Kim's sales account on 31 July 2024?
   - **A** Credit $4 000
   - **B** Credit $4 500
   - **C** Debit $4 000
   - **D** Debit $4 500 *[1 mark]*

3 Lalita, a sole trader, maintains a complete set of books of prime entry.

   Which book is written up from credit notes received?
   - **A** Purchases journal
   - **B** Sales journal
   - **C** Purchases returns journal
   - **D** Sales returns journal *[1 mark]*

4 Fatima, a sole trader, purchases inventory for $800. She is allowed a trade discount of 5 per cent and a cash discount of 10 per cent.

   Which amount will be entered into Fatima's purchases account?
   - **A** $680
   - **B** $684
   - **C** $720
   - **D** $760 *[1 mark]*

5 Kim Jun returned inventory to her supplier, Jason. It was recorded in Jason's books of prime entry.

   Which account should be debited in Jason's general ledger?
   - **A** Purchases
   - **B** Purchases returns
   - **C** Sales
   - **D** Sales returns *[1 mark]*

5 Books of prime entry

6 Which of the following combinations is a typical advantage and disadvantage of digital accounting?

  A Greater accuracy; limited analytical capabilities

  B Lower long-term costs; limited security

  C More control; overdependence on technology

  D Scalability; high training costs

[1 mark]

7 Identify two books of prime entry which a trader may keep other than a general journal. In each case, identify a source document for that book. The first one has been completed as an example. *[2 marks]*

Book of prime entry	Source document
Purchases journal	Purchases invoice

8 State one reason why a trader might use books of prime entry. *[1 mark]*

....

9 Identify two accounts to which totals from a three-column cash book are posted. *[2 marks]*

....

10 State **two** uses of source documents. *[2 marks]*

....

....

11 Liam maintains a purchases journal, a purchase returns journal, a sales journal and a sales returns journal. Identify one other book of prime entry which he may maintain. *[1 mark]*

....

12 Discuss the challenges a business might face when transitioning from manual to digital accounting. *[3 marks]*

....

....

....

13 On 1 October, Basant and Yeshwant owe Shalini $160 and $250 respectively. Shalini's sales and sales returns journal for the month showed the following.

Shalini's sales journal		
		$
Oct 5	Basant	400
Oct 17	Yeshwant	370
		770

Shalini's sales returns journal		
		$
Oct 10	Basant	110
Oct 27	Yeshwant	70
		180

2 SOURCES AND RECORDING OF DATA

Prepare the following ledger accounts in Shalini's books for October. Balance the accounts where necessary and bring down the balances on 1 November. You can copy the ledgers below.

Basant's account						
Date	Details	$	Date	Details	$

[5 marks]

Sales account						
Date	Details	$	Date	Details	$

[1 mark]

Sales returns account						
Date	Details	$	Date	Details	$

[1 mark]

14 Basil maintains a cash book with columns for bank and cash and discounts. He had the following balances on 1 September 2024: Bank $4 000 (Dr); Cash $2 500; Johnny $500 (Dr); Jenny $900 (Dr).

The following transactions took place during September.

- Sep 3 – Basil sold goods, $300, for cash to Bikram
- Sep 10 – Basil wrote a cheque for his personal use $60
- Sep 15 – Johnny paid Basil $460 by cheque in full settlement
- Sep 16 – Basil paid $250 of the cash in the till into the bank
- Sep 18 – Basil paid a credit supplier, Ali, $665 by credit transfer in full settlement after receiving a discount of 5 per cent.
- Sep 20 – Basil withdrew $320 cash from the bank for office use
- Sep 25 – $864 was received by credit transfer from Jenny, a credit customer, in full settlement of her debt
- Sep 28 – Cash sales banked $270

a Prepare Basil's cash book for September. Balance the cash and bank columns and bring down the balances on 1 October. [15 marks]

b State the type of discount given on 25 September. [1 mark]

....

c Calculate the discount rate given on 25 September. [2 marks]

....

2 SOURCES AND RECORDING OF DATA

d Identify the transactions which are known as contra entries. Explain why they are known as contra entries. *[4 marks]*

....

....

....

e Prepare the following general ledger accounts in Basil's books to show the posting of the totals of the discount columns from the cash book. You can copy the ledgers below. *[2 marks]*

i) Discounts allowed account

Date	Details	$	Date	Details	$

ii) Discounts received account

Date	Details	$	Date	Details	$

15 Sangita maintains both a three-column cash book and a petty cash book. She maintains the petty cash book on the imprest system with an imprest amount of $250.

She supplied the following information for the month ended 31 August 2025.

Date	Details	$
Aug 1	Petty cash balance	19
Aug 1	Petty cash restored to imprest amount	
Aug 3	Paid taxi fares	24
Aug 6	Paid for parcel post	10
Aug 8	An employee returned a loan received out of petty cash in July	16
Aug 15	Paid Mansi, a credit supplier	17
Aug 20	Paid for office cleaning supplies	10

a State one advantage of using the imprest system of petty cash. *[1 mark]*

....

b State one reason for maintaining a petty cash book and a main cash book. *[1 mark]*

....

c i) Complete Sangita's petty cash book on the next page.

ii) Balance the petty cash book and bring down the balance on 1 September 2025.

iii) Enter the amount required on 1 September 2025 to restore the petty cash to the imprest amount. *[10 marks]*

5 Books of prime entry

Sangita's petty cash book

Receipts	Date	Details	Total paid	Postage	Travel	Sundries	Ledger accounts
$	2025		$	$	$	$	$

2 SOURCES AND RECORDING OF DATA

d Explain how the double entry will be completed for the items shown in the postage column of the petty cash book. *[2 marks]*

....

16 a State three uses of the general journal. *[3 marks]*

....

....

....

b Prepare journal entries to record the following on 31 December 2025. Narratives are required. You can copy the journals below.

   i) Electricity for the year is $5 700, which includes a prepayment of $600. *[3 marks]*

Date	Details	Debit	Credit
2025		$	$

   ii) Provide for depreciation of equipment $400. *[3 marks]*

Date	Details	Debit	Credit
2025		$	$

   iii) Closing inventory was $20 000. *[3 marks]*

Date	Details	Debit	Credit
2025		$	$

   iv) Make an allowance for irrecoverable debts of $200. *[3 marks]*

Date	Details	Debit	Credit
2025		$	$

5 Books of prime entry

v) Opening inventory on 1 January 2025 was valued at $10 000. *[3 marks]*

Date	Details	Debit	Credit
2025		$	$

vi) Returned faulty furniture, bought on credit from Ace Furniture, $2 500. *[3 marks]*

Date	Details	Debit	Credit
2025		$	$

17 Ubertus keeps his petty cash book on the imprest system with an imprest amount of $200. At 31 July there were vouchers for petty cash expenditure totalling $134.50 in the petty cash box. He had not claimed a taxi fare of $11.30.

Calculate the amount remaining in the petty cash box after Ubertus has claimed his taxi fare. Show your workings. *[2 marks]*

....

....

....

3 Verification of accounting records

Student's Book Chapters 6–9

6 The trial balance

1 A sole trader's trial balance total on the credit side was $7 000 more than the total on the debit side. Which error caused this?

    A A credit entry of $3 500 was incorrectly posted as a debit entry.

    B A debit entry of $3 500 was incorrectly posted as a credit entry.

    C Drawings of $7 000 were omitted entirely from the books.

    D Repairs to motor vehicle of $7 000 was debited to the motor van account. *[1 mark]*

2 Which error is revealed by a trial balance?

    A Arithmetical error

    B Error of commission

    C Error of original entry

    D Error of principle *[1 mark]*

3 Which is an error of original entry?

    A A cheque received from S. Tilly was credited to T. Tilly's account.

    B A purchases invoice, $540, entered in the sales journal as $450.

    C The purchase of machinery was debited to the bank account and credited to the machinery account.

    D Wages paid debited to the property account. *[1 mark]*

4 The cost of machinery repairs was debited to the machinery account.

How would this affect the profit and the non-current assets? *[1 mark]*

	Profit for the year		Non-current assets	
	Overstated	Understated	Overstated	Understated
A		✓		✓
B	✓		✓	
C	✓			✓
D		✓	✓	

5 Define the following:

    a A trial balance *[1 mark]*

....

....

    b Closing inventory *[1 mark]*

....

....

6 Give two uses of a trial balance. *[2 marks]*

....

....

7 State one limitation of a trial balance. *[1 mark]*

....

8 An inexperienced book-keeper prepared the following trial balance, which contains errors.

Prepare a corrected trial balance on 31 July 2025. You can copy the trial balance template below. *[7 marks]*

Gaurav
Trial balance at 31 July 2025

	Debit $	Credit $
Owner's equity	40 000	
Cash		170
Bank overdraft	300	
Trade receivables	500	
Trade payables	700	
Property and buildings		28 520
Machinery		7 000
Inventory at 1 August 2024		1 000
Purchases		760
Sales	2 000	
Returns outwards		50
Returns inwards	200	
Salaries		500
Interest received	600	
Rent		2 000
Inventory at 31 July 2025		4 500
Furniture and fixtures	3 000	
	47 300	44 500

Gaurav
Corrected trial balance at 31 July 2025

	Debit $	Credit $

3 VERIFICATION OF ACCOUNTING RECORDS

7 Correction of errors

1. Corinne, who owns a hair salon, prepared a trial balance. She had omitted the salaries account, $500, and had entered the balance of the rent account as $7 000 instead of $700.

   What was the balance of the suspense account?

   A $5 800 credit

   B $5 800 debit

   C $6 500 credit

   D $6 500 debit [1 mark]

2. A trial balance does not balance. What caused the error?

   A A. Brown account was debited instead of B. Brown account

   B An entry was completely omitted

   C An entry was made in only one account

   D Purchases account was debited instead of motor vehicles account [1 mark]

3. Suman, a sole trader, discovers that cash received from Thangam, a credit customer, has been recorded as a cash sale. [1 mark]

   Which of these entries will correct the error?

	Account debited	Account credited
A	Cash	Sales
B	Sales	Cash
C	Sales	Thangam
D	Thangam	Cash

4. After which error will a trial balance still balance?

   A An error in adding up a trade payable's account

   B An error in entering an item on an invoice

   C An error in extracting the balance of the salary account

   D An error in recording cash received in the cash book [1 mark]

5. A trial balance does not agree. The credit column totals $9 000. Two errors are then found:

   - The sales journal has been undercast by $200.
   - Sales to Yolanda, $300, on credit, have been incorrectly debited to Yeni's account.

   What is the total of the debit column of the trial balance?

   A $8 600

   B $8 800

   C $9 200

   D $9 400 [1 mark]

6. a Explain two types of error that affect the trial balance. [4 marks]

   ....

   ....

   b Explain what is meant by an error of complete reversal. [2 marks]

   ....

   ....

   c Explain what is meant by an error of principle. [2 marks]

   ....

   ....

7 Correction of errors

7 After the preparation of a sole trader's statement of profit or loss, the following errors and omissions were discovered:

   i) Trade receivables amounted to $14 900 on 31 December 2024. This included a debt of $700, which is irrecoverable.

   ii) An allowance for irrecoverable debts of 3 per cent of the remaining trade receivables should have been created.

   iii) No entry had been made for returns outwards of $800.

   iv) Inventory on 31 December 2024 included goods, $4 000, which were damaged and expected to be sold for $2 700.

Complete the following table to show the effect of correcting errors 1–4 on the profit for the year ended 31 December 2024. Where there is no effect, write 'no effect'. *[4 marks]*

Error	Effect on profit for the year		
	Increase $	Decrease $	No effect
i)		700	
ii)		426	
iii)	800		
iv)		1 300	

8 No adjustment was made for annual salaries paid by cheque when preparing the financial statements. Identify the effect of this error by placing a tick (✓) in the correct box(es). *[2 marks]*

Profit for the year is overstated	✓
Profit for the year is understated	
Current assets are overstated	✓
Current assets are understated	
Non-current assets are understated	
Non-current assets are overstated	

9 Holly bought inventory, $350, on credit from Nelly. This was recorded in Holly's books as $530.

   a Identify the type of error which has been made. *[1 mark]*

   Error of original entry

   b Prepare the journal entry required to correct this error. A narrative is not required. *[2 marks]*

	Debit $	Credit $
Nelly	180	
Purchases		180

3 VERIFICATION OF ACCOUNTING RECORDS

10 State **two** reasons why a suspense account is opened when a trial balance does not agree.

1. To make the totals of the trial balance agree temporarily so that the difference can be investigated.

2. To enable the preparation of the financial statements to continue until the errors causing the difference are found and corrected.

11

a State the double entry needed to correct error i).

Debit entry	$	Credit entry	$
Sales	200	Ted (trade receivables)	200

b Suspense account

Details	$	Details	$
Balance b/d (difference on trial balance)	512	Heat and light	612
Insurance	100		
	612		**612**

c No, Kriti cannot be sure that all errors have been found. The suspense account and trial balance only reveal errors that affect the agreement of the trial balance. Errors such as errors of omission, commission, principle, original entry, complete reversal and compensating errors do not affect the agreement of the trial balance and so would not be detected.

8 Bank reconciliation

1 On 31 December, Devon's bank statement shows a credit balance of $6 000 and the cash book shows a debit balance of $5 400. There is a receipt in the cash book of $400, which does not appear on the bank statement.

What is the amount of unpresented cheques?

- A $1 000
- B $1 400
- C $1 600
- D $2 000 *[1 mark]*

2 Chantel's bank statement shows a balance of $1 500 (debit) at 31 July. The following items did not appear in the bank statement during the month, although they were recorded in the cash book:

	$
Cheques issued	5 000
Cheques deposited	9 500

What was the balance in the cash book at 31 July?

- A $3 000 credit
- B $3 000 debit
- C $6 000 credit
- D $6 000 debit *[1 mark]*

3 Kamil receives a cheque for $300, records it in his cash book and banks it on the same day. A statement sent by the bank that day does not show this $300.

How is this $300 shown on the bank reconciliation statement?

- A As an uncredited deposit added to the balance as per cash book
- B As an uncredited deposit deducted from the balance as per cash book
- C As an unpresented cheque added to the balance as per cash book
- D As an unpresented cheque deducted from the balance as per cash book *[1 mark]*

4 Isabel prepares a bank reconciliation statement after updating her cash book.

What is shown in the bank reconciliation statement?

- A Bank charges debited in the bank statement
- B Cheques credited in the bank statement in error
- C Direct debits directly paid by the bank
- D Dividends received directly credited to the bank *[1 mark]*

5 Wilma's bank statement shows a credit balance at bank of $4 700. The amount of unpresented cheques is $2 000 and the amount of uncredited deposits is $800.

What is the debit balance in the cash book?

- A $3 500
- B $5 500
- C $5 900
- D $6 700 *[1 mark]*

6 How does real-time data access benefit businesses in digital banking?

- A It allows for immediate spotting and correction of discrepancies.
- B It delays the identification of unusual transactions.
- C It increases reliance on physical records.
- D It prevents all technical issues.

3 VERIFICATION OF ACCOUNTING RECORDS

7 Nonaki, a sole trader, has received his bank statement. The following items have not yet been entered into his cash book. Complete the following table by placing a tick (✓) to show whether the item will increase, reduce or have no effect on the debit balance in his cash book. *[3 marks]*

	Increase	Decrease	Have no effect
Bank charges			
Credit transfer			
Customer's cheque dishonoured			

8 Salim sells goods for cash and on credit. He pays the cheques received from his credit customers into the bank on the day he receives them. He collects the cash receipts in a cash safe and pays the total into his bank account each month.

On 1 March 2025, Salim's cash book showed a debit bank balance of $3 500.

Salim's transactions for the month of March 2025 were:

Date March	Details	$
2	Received a cheque from Lala, a credit customer	400
6	Purchased goods from Bishwas, paying by cheque	1 100
8	Sold goods on credit to Malika	2 700
10	Paid salaries by bank transfer	500
15	Received a cheque from Anton	1 780
20	Paid Arden by cheque	900
31	Cash sales for the month of March	4 600

a Prepare the bank columns of Salim's cash book to record the above transactions. Balance the cash book and bring down the balance on 1 April 2025. You can copy the cash book below. *[5 marks]*

Salim
Cash book (bank columns only)

Date	Details	$	Date	Details	$

At 31 March. Salim had recorded the cash sales in his cash book but had yet to deposit it in the bank. The cheque paid to Arden dated 20 March was not cleared by the bank until 2 April.

The bank statement at 31 March showed a credit balance at the bank of $4 080.

b Prepare a bank reconciliation statement for Salim at 31 March 2025. You can copy the statement below. *[5 marks]*

Salim
Bank reconciliation statement at 31 March 2025

	$	$

c Explain why debit entries in the cash book appear as credit entries in the bank statement and vice versa. *[2 marks]*

....

....

....

....

....

....

9 Define the following:

a Dishonoured cheque *[1 mark]*

....

....

b Bank overdraft *[1 mark]*

....

....

10 Discuss the possible challenges for a business in preparing bank reconciliation in a digital banking environment. *[3 marks]*

....

....

....

11 Logan is a sole trader. On 20 April 2025, he received the following bank statement.

Date	Details	Debit	Credit	Balance
2025		$	$	$
Apr 1	Balance b/d		460	460(cr)
Apr 7	Kelsey		1 300	1 760(cr)
Apr 10	Henry industries	600		1 160(cr)
Apr 15	Interest	60		1 100(cr)
Apr 20	Credit transfer (dividends)		400	1 500(cr)

a Copy and complete Logan's cash book on 20 April. Balance the cash book on that date. *[3 marks]*

Logan's cash book (bank columns only)					
Date	Details	$	Date	Details	$
2025			2025		
Apr 1	Balance b/d	460	Apr 14	Henry industries	600
Apr 9	Kelsey	1 300	Apr 18	Kairu	780
Apr 19	Yuki	680			

3 VERIFICATION OF ACCOUNTING RECORDS

b Prepare the bank reconciliation statement at 20 April 2025. *[4 marks]*

Bank reconciliation statement at 20 April 2025		
	$	$

9 Control accounts

1 Sam maintains a control account for his purchases ledger.

   What is the purpose of this control account?

   A To calculate the amount owed to customers

   B To calculate total purchases

   C To check the accuracy of the purchases ledger

   D To make the trial balance totals agree *[1 mark]*

2 Mischner, a sole trader, prepares control accounts to monitor her sales and purchases ledgers.

   What would appear in Mischner's sales ledger control account?

   A Cash sales

   B Discounts received

   C Refunds to credit customers

   D Returns outward *[1 mark]*

3 Roger, a sole trader, provided the following information:

2024		$
May 1	Trade receivables	8 000
May 31	Total of sales journal	9 000
May 31	Total of sales returns journal	600
May 31	Cash book: cash from trade receivables	5 000

What is the total of trade receivables at the end of June?

A $11 400   **C** $22 600

B $21 400   **D** $28 600   *[1 mark]*

4 Corey's sales ledger control account had a balance of $90 000 at the beginning and $76 000 at the end of the month. The credit sales were $56 000.

   How much did Corey receive from his trade receivables during the month?

   A $14 000   **C** $70 000

   B $34 000   **D** $110 000   *[1 mark]*

5 Sung Jin's purchases ledger control account has a credit balance of $1 450.

   What is the balance after entering the discount received, $25, and interest charged on an overdue account, $60?

   A $1 415   **C** $1 485

   B $1 475   **D** $1 510   *[1 mark]*

6 Which of the following is **not** a built-in security feature of digital systems?

   A Access controls

   B Automated reconciliation

   C Password protection

   D Encryption   *[1 mark]*

7 Mitchel employs a book-keeper to maintain the accounts of his credit customers.

   Identify the account Mitchel prepares to check for fraud or error in the book-keeper's work. *[1 mark]*

....

9 Control accounts

8 Alena is a sole trader who does not keep double entry records. However, the following information is available from the records:

	1 Jun 2023	31 May 2024
	$	$
Trade payables	7 900	5 700
Trade receivables	8 200	7 600
Inventory	6 300	5 200

- All sales and purchases are made on a credit basis.
- Receipts from trade receivables during the year ended 31 May 2024 amounted to $37 600.
- Payments to trade payables during the year ended 31 May 2024 amounted to $29 500.

a Calculate the total sales for the year ended 31 May 2024. You can copy the ledger below. *[3 marks]*

Sales ledger control account				
Date	Details	$	Date	Details	$

b Calculate the total purchases for the year ended 31 May 2024. You can copy the ledger below. *[3 marks]*

Purchases ledger control account				
Date	Details	$	Date	Details	$

c Explain two ways Alena can use control accounts in her business. *[4 marks]*

....

....

....

....

d Suggest one limitation of the usefulness of control accounts in Alena's approach to record keeping. *[1 mark]*

....

....

3 VERIFICATION OF ACCOUNTING RECORDS

9 Give the source for each entry in the sales ledger control account. *[11 marks]*

Entries in the sales ledger control account	Source of the entries
Balance b/d	
Sales	
Cash	
Bank	
Sale returns	
Irrecoverable debts	
Discounts allowed	
Dishonoured cheques	
Refunds to trade receivables	
Interest charged on overdue accounts	
Balance c/d	

9 Control accounts

10 Sumit is a trader. He provides the following information.

	$
At 1 January 2024:	
Sales ledger balance (dr)	9 760
Sales ledger balance (cr)	27
Purchases ledger balance (dr)	16
Purchases ledger balance (cr)	6 270
For the year ended 31 December 2024:	
Credit sales	78 205
Returns from credit customers	1 121
Credit purchases	54 209
Returns to credit suppliers	764
Receipts from credit customers	69 600
Payments to credit suppliers	51 926
Refund from a credit supplier	330
Discount allowed	1 418
Discount received	1 061
Irrecoverable debt written off	116
Interest charged by a credit supplier on an overdue account	61
At 1 January 2025:	
Sales ledger balance (dr)	?
Sales ledger balance (cr)	117
Purchases ledger balance (dr)	54
Purchases ledger balance (cr)	?

Additional information:

- A set off (contra entry) of $405 was made in June 2024 between the sales and purchases ledgers.
- The receipts from credit customers included a cheque for $302 returned by the bank as unpaid in December 2024.
- All receipts and payments were either by cheque or by credit transfer.

a Suggest two possible reasons why some sales ledger accounts had credit balances. *[2 marks]*

....

....

3 VERIFICATION OF ACCOUNTING RECORDS

b Prepare the sales ledger control account for the year ended 31 December 2024. You can copy the ledger below.

[11 marks]

Sales ledger control account						
Date	Details	$	Date	Details	$

c Prepare the purchases ledger control account for the year ended 31 December 2024. You can copy the ledger below.

[11 marks]

Purchases ledger control account						
Date	Details	$	Date	Details	$

d Advise Sumit whether he should start charging interest on overdue customers' accounts. Justify your answer.

[5 marks]

....

....

....

....

....

....

4 Accounting procedures

Student's Book Chapters 10–14

10 Capital and revenue expenditure and receipts

1 Hari, an inexperienced accountant, treated capital expenditure as revenue expenditure. What is the effect on the financial statements?

   A Current assets are undervalued
   B Non-current assets are overstated
   C Profit for the year is increased
   D Profit for the year is reduced *[1 mark]*

2 On 30 June 2024, ABC Engineering received an invoice showing the following:

2024		$
Jun 6	Cost of equipment	40 000
	Cost of installation of equipment	2 500
Jun 26	Cost of repairs	1 000
	Cost of replacement parts	400

   How much was the capital expenditure?

   A $40 000 **C** $42 500
   B $40 400 **D** $42 900 *[1 mark]*

3 Jahangir, a sole trader, bought a printer for his business. He sold the printer after one year on 31 July 2024. How would the proceeds of the sale be classified?

   A Capital expenditure
   B Capital receipt
   C Revenue expenditure
   D Revenue receipt *[1 mark]*

4 Sandie, a sole trader, paid $30 000 for a new motor van. The invoice she received from the dealer showed the following:

	$
Motor van	30 000
Number plates	200
Insurance for 36 months	3 600

   How much was the capital expenditure?

   A $30 000 **C** $33 600
   B $30 200 **D** $33 800 *[1 mark]*

5 Define the following:

   a Capital expenditure *[1 mark]*

   ....

   ....

   b Revenue expenditure *[1 mark]*

   ....

   ....

   c Capital receipts *[1 mark]*

   ....

   ....

   d Revenue receipts *[1 mark]*

   ....

   ....

4 ACCOUNTING PROCEDURES

6 Identify whether the following statements are true or false by writing 'true' or 'false' against each statement in the following table. *[10 marks]*

	True/False
Revenue expenditure is the amount a business spends to acquire, improve or extend the life of non-current assets.	
Capital expenditure is non-recurring by nature.	
Revenue expenditure is shown in the statement of financial position of a business.	
Industries such as telecommunications have high levels of capital expenditure.	
Revenue expenditure is a short-term expense incurred to meet the operational costs of running the business on a day-to-day basis.	
Revenue expenditure is meant to extend a business ability to earn income.	
The one-off costs incurred in acquiring non-current assets should be included as capital expenditure.	
Capital expenditure is charged to profit in the statement of profit or loss as soon as it is incurred.	
Revenue expenditure is meant to maintain the business ability to operate.	
Businesses must spread the cost of a non-current asset over the years the asset is used.	

7 Vivien owns a hair salon. Complete the following table by placing a tick (✓) in the correct column to identify whether each item is capital or revenue expenditure. *[5 marks]*

	Capital expenditure	Revenue expenditure
Employees' wages		
New mirrors for salon		
Installation of new mirrors for salon		
Purchase of shampoo		
Purchase of hair driers		

8 Complete the following table by placing a tick (✓) in the correct column to identify whether each item is a capital or revenue receipt. *[4 marks]*

	Capital receipt	Revenue receipt
A loan taken from a bank		
Fees received by a service business		
Rent received		
An issue of shares		
Sales revenue received by a trading or manufacturing business		

9 Xavier prepared his draft financial statements. These showed a draft profit for the year of $17 620 and a draft total assets value of $51 204. The following errors were then discovered.

   i) A payment of $400 for car insurance had been treated as capital expenditure.
   ii) The receipt of $2 000 from a new bank loan had been credited to sales.
   iii) New machinery costing $1 050 had been treated as revenue expenditure.

Calculate corrected profit and total assets values by entering the necessary adjustments in the table below. *[8 marks]*

	Profit for the year	Total assets
	$	$
Draft values	17 620	51 204
Error i)		
Error ii)		
Error iii)		
Corrected values		

11 Accounting for depreciation and disposal of non-current assets

1. Yagmur bought a motor van for $20 000 and depreciated it at the rate of 20 per cent per annum on the reducing balance basis. What was the net book value at the end of the second year?
   - A $7 200
   - B $8 000
   - C $12 000
   - D $12 800 *[1 mark]*

2. What is the effect of providing depreciation?
   - A It helps in extending the life of non-current assets
   - B It increases the current assets of a business
   - C It increases profit for the year
   - D It reduces profit for the year *[1 mark]*

3. Which assets should best be depreciated using the revaluation method?
   - A Equipment
   - B Loose tools
   - C Motor vehicle
   - D Property *[1 mark]*

4. When an asset is sold for a price lower than its net book value, which of the following entries is made to record the loss on disposal?
   - A Cash book (Dr) / Disposal account (Cr)
   - B Disposal account (Dr) / Cash book (Cr)
   - C Disposal account (Dr) / Statement of profit or loss (Cr)
   - D Statement of profit or loss (Dr) / Disposal account (Cr) *[1 mark]*

5. Julie bought a motor vehicle on 1 January 2021 for $30 000 and depreciated it by 20 per cent per annum using the reducing balance method. She sold the motor vehicle on 1 January 2024 for $4 000. What was the profit or loss on disposal?
   - A $8 000 loss
   - B $8 000 profit
   - C $11 360 loss
   - D $11 360 profit *[1 mark]*

6. A vehicle was bought for $30 000 on 1 January. Two years later, the vehicle had a book value of $27 000. Depreciation was calculated using the straight-line method.

   What is the annual rate of depreciation?
   - A 3%
   - B 5%
   - C 10%
   - D 25% *[1 mark]*

4 ACCOUNTING PROCEDURES

7 Non-current assets depreciate for various reasons, including wear and tear. State two other reasons why assets depreciate. *[2 marks]*

....

....

8 a Explain the straight-line method of depreciation. *[2 marks]*

....

....

....

b Describe the circumstances when the straight-line method of depreciation may be used. *[1 mark]*

....

c Explain the reducing balance method of depreciation. *[2 marks]*

....

....

....

d Describe the circumstances when the reducing balance method of depreciation may be used. *[1 mark]*

....

....

e State which of the two methods of depreciation, straight-line or reducing balance, would be most appropriate for each of the following non-current assets. Give your reason.

   i) Property *[2 marks]*

   Method: ....

   Reason: ....

   ii) Motor vehicle *[2 marks]*

   Method: ....

   Reason: ....

   iii) Computer equipment *[2 marks]*

   Method: ....

   Reason: ....

f Explain the revaluation method of depreciation. *[2 marks]*

....

....

....

g Describe the circumstances when the revaluation method of depreciation may be used. *[1 mark]*

....

....

....

h Suggest two assets that may be depreciated in this way. *[2 marks]*

....

9 A business provides for the depreciation of its non-current assets. State the effect of this on:

a Profit for the year *[1 mark]*

....

b Net book value of non-current assets *[1 mark]*

....

10 Pamela is planning to buy some office furniture costing $6 000. She estimates the furniture will have an economic life of three years and a scrap value of $1 000 after that time. She decided to depreciate the furniture using the reducing balance method at 30 per cent per annum.

a Calculate the depreciation to be charged on the furniture for each of the three years of its economic life. Show your workings for each year.

  i) Year one *[1 mark]*

....

  ii) Year two *[1 mark]*

....

  iii) Year three *[1 mark]*

....

b Complete the following extract from Pamela's statement of financial position at the end of the third year. *[3 marks]*

Pamela				
Statement of financial position (extract)				
Non-current assets		Cost	Provision for depreciation	Net book value
		$	$	$

c Pamela compared the calculated net book value of the computer system after three years with its expected scrap value after three years, $1 000. State whether the business should use a higher or lower percentage rate to calculate depreciation. Give a reason for your answer. *[2 marks]*

....

....

....

4 ACCOUNTING PROCEDURES

11 Angus Recanni is a sole trader whose financial year ends on 31 December. He uses the straight-line method of depreciation at the rate of 10 per cent per annum calculated from the date of purchase of the non-current asset.

His ledger balances on 1 January 2024 included the following:

	$
Machinery at cost	14 000
Provision for depreciation of machinery	2 800

- On 30 June 2024, machinery which had cost $4 000 on 1 January 2022 was sold for $300 cash.
- On 1 July 2024, machinery costing $5 000 was purchased by bank transfer from ABC Machines.

Prepare the following accounts in the ledger of Angus Recanni for the year ended 31 December 2024. Balance the accounts where necessary and bring down the balances on 1 January 2025.

Angus Recanni
Machinery account

Date	Details	$	Date	Details	$

[5 marks]

Provision for depreciation – Machinery account

Date	Details	$	Date	Details	$

[5 marks]

Disposal of machinery account

Date	Details	$	Date	Details	$

[5 marks]

12 State **two** reasons why a business provides for depreciation. *[2 marks]*

....

....

....

13 Freddy is a trader. He calculated his depreciation charge for the year ended 31 December 2024 on his machinery at $1 245.

  a Prepare the journal entry to record the depreciation of machinery for the year ended 31 December 2024. A narrative is required. You can copy the journal below. *[3 marks]*

General journal				
Date	Details		Debit $	Credit $

Additional information:

- On 31 December 2024, Freddy sold a motor vehicle for $3 100 cash. This vehicle originally cost $7 000; by the date of sale, its accumulated depreciation amounted to $3 300.

  b Prepare the journal entry to record the sale of the motor vehicle. A narrative is required. You can copy the journal below. *[9 marks]*

General journal				
Date	Details		Debit $	Credit $

12 Other payables and other receivables

1 Paul, a sole trader, has not adjusted accrued insurance in his financial statements. What is the effect of this omission? *[1 mark]*

	Profit for the year	Current liabilities
A	Overstated	Overstated
B	Overstated	Understated
C	Understated	Overstated
D	Understated	Understated

4 ACCOUNTING PROCEDURES

2 Gerda, a sole trader, prepared her financial statements for the year ended 31 December 2024. A debit balance was brought down in the rent account.

What does this debit balance represent?

A Rent for the year ended 31 December 2024

B Rent owing for the year ended 31 December 2024

C Rent paid during the year ended 31 December 2024

D Rent paid for the year ended 31 December 2025 *[1 mark]*

3 George's statement of profit or loss for the year ended 30 June 2024 revealed that his business had a loss of $12 000. After a check of his accounting records for the year, he found the following error:

Rent $670, prepaid for the year ended 30 June 2025, had been included as an expense in his statement of profit or loss for the year ended 30 June 2024.

What is George's corrected loss for the year?

A $11 033

B $11 330

C $12 670

D $12 760 *[1 mark]*

4 The opening balances on the commission receivable account for two years ended 31 December 2024 and 2025 are given below:

	$
1 January 2024	1 500 dr
1 January 2025	800 cr

$6 000 commission was received in cash and bank transfers during the year ended 31 December 2024.

What amount should be shown for commission receivable in the statement of profit or loss for the year ended 31 December 2024?

A $3 700

B $4 500

C $6 000

D $6 800 *[1 mark]*

5 Sneh, a sole trader, had prepaid one months' rent on 1 June 2024. During the year, rent was paid in cash. On 31 May 2025, two months' rent was owing. How does Sneh calculate the rent expense for the year ended 31 May 2025?

A Opening prepayment + cash paid − closing balance

B Opening prepayment + cash paid + closing balance

C Opening prepayment − cash paid + closing balance

D Opening balance − cash paid − closing balance *[1 mark]*

6 What is the journal entry to adjust for prepaid income at year-end?

A Dr Other receivables, Cr Income account

B Dr Income account, Cr Other receivables

C Dr Income account, Cr Other payables

D Dr Other payables, Cr Income account *[1 mark]*

7 Mala, a sole trader, receives an electricity bill each month for electricity used. At 31 January 2025, $60 for electricity used in January was still unpaid. During the months of February and March, she made the following payments by bank transfer to her electricity provider:

	$
15 February 2025	110
8 March 2025	85

12 Other payables and other receivables

On 31 March 2025, Mala received a bill for $56 for electricity used in March.

a Explain the meaning of the accounting concept of matching. *[2 marks]*

....

....

....

b Prepare the electricity account in Mala's general ledger for February and March 2025. Show the amount transferred to Mala's statement of profit or loss for each month. Balance the account and bring down the balance on 1 April 2025. You can copy the ledger below. *[7 marks]*

Mala's general ledger Electricity account					
Date	Details	$	Date	Details	$

8 a Identify the section of the statement of financial position in which rent received in advance would appear. *[1 mark]*

....

b Identify the accounting concept applied when an adjustment is made for a prepaid expense. *[1 mark]*

....

c Richard is a sole trader. His general expenses account for the year ended 31 December 2024 showed the following:

2024		$
Jan 1	Opening balance	2 690 (cr)
Jan 1–Dec 31	Cash payments made	10 900
Dec 31	Closing balance	2 500 (cr)

Calculate the general expenses shown in Richard's statement of profit or loss for the year ended 31 December 2024. Show your workings. You can copy the ledger below. *[4 marks]*

Richard's general ledger General expenses account					
Date	Details	$	Date	Details	$

4 ACCOUNTING PROCEDURES

9 Vijay, a sole trader, provided the following information regarding his stationery expenses for the year ended 31 May 2025.

Vijay
Stationery account

Date	Details	$	Date	Details	$
2024			2024		
Jun 1	J.B. Office Supplies	560			
2025			2025		
			May 31	Statement of profit or loss	480
				Balance c/d	80
		560			560
Jun 1	Balance b/d	80			

a Identify the amount paid for stationery during the year. *[1 mark]*

....

b Identify the amount recorded as stationery expenses in the statement of profit or loss for the year ended 31 May 2025. *[1 mark]*

....

c State what is represented by the closing balance of $80 at the end of the financial year. *[1 mark]*

....

d Identify the financial statement in which the $80 will be recorded. Give a reason for your answer.
Name of the financial statement: *[1 mark]*

....

Reason: *[1 mark]*

....

....

10 Daniel started his business on 1 January 2024, when he paid $1 500 for insurance for the 15 months to 31 March 2025.

During his first year of trading, he received a commission of $17 100. Of this, $2 000 was received in advance for the work done during 2024.

a Prepare the journal entry to record the transfer of the insurance expense for the year ended 31 December 2024 to the statement of profit or loss. A narrative is not required. *[2 marks]*

	General journal		
Date	Details	Debit $	Credit $

46 **Photocopying prohibited**

b Prepare the journal entry to record the transfer of the commission receivable for the year ended 31 December 2024 to the statement of profit or loss. A narrative is not required. *[2 marks]*

General journal			
Date	Details	Debit $	Credit $

13 Irrecoverable debts and allowance for irrecoverable debts

1 Bala maintains a sales ledger control account and an allowance for irrecoverable debts account. On 1 June 2025, the balances were:

	$
Sales ledger control account	24 580
Allowance for irrecoverable debts account	1 229

What is the percentage rate used for the allowance for irrecoverable debts? *[1 mark]*

A 2.5%   C 5.5%
B 5%   D 10%

2 Ramesh owes $4 000 to Divesh. He pays 95 per cent of the debt. Divesh writes off the remaining debts as irrecoverable. What entry will Divesh make to record the writing off of the irrecoverable debt? *[1 mark]*

	Account debited	$	Account credited	$
A	Irrecoverable debt	200	Ramesh	200
B	Ramesh	200	Irrecoverable debt	200
C	Irrecoverable debt	4 000	Ramesh	4 000
D	Ramesh	4 000	Irrecoverable debt	4 000

3 Phara maintains an allowance for irrecoverable debts of 5 per cent of her trade receivables. Her trade receivables amounted to $16 000 on 1 April 2024 and $22 000 on 31 March 2025.

What is the amount of the increase in Phara's allowance for irrecoverable debts on 31 March 2025?

A $300   C $3 000
B $600   D $6 000   *[1 mark]*

4 Hyung Ho is a trader. He wrote off the balance on a customer's account as an irrecoverable debt in June 2024. Where will this irrecoverable debt appear in Hyung Ho's financial statements prepared at 31 December 2024?

A As a deduction from creditors in the statement of financial position
B As a deduction from purchases in the trading section of the statement of profit or loss
C As a deduction from sales in the trading section of the statement of profit or loss
D As an expense in the section of the statement of profit or loss   *[1 mark]*

4 ACCOUNTING PROCEDURES

5 Alex, a sole trader, maintains a full set of accounting records. He provides for irrecoverable debts at 5 per cent of closing trade receivables.

a On 31 March 2018, the balance on the allowance for irrecoverable debts in his books had increased from $1 000 to $1 400. Suggest one reason for the increase. *[1 mark]*

....

b Prepare the journal entry to record the change in the allowance for irrecoverable debts. A narrative is required. You can copy the journal below. *[3 marks]*

Alex General journal		
	Debit	Credit
	$	$

c Explain one accounting principle which is applied when an allowance for irrecoverable debts is maintained. *[2 marks]*

....

....

....

....

6 Suggest four ways a business can avoid irrecoverable debts. *[4 marks]*

....

....

....

....

7 State two ways in which an estimate of the amount of the allowance for irrecoverable debts can be made. *[2 marks]*

....

....

....

8 a Explain what is meant by the following terms.

   i) Irrecoverable debt *[2 marks]*

....

....

13 Irrecoverable debts and allowance for irrecoverable debts

ii) Recovery of irrecoverable debts [2 marks]

....

....

b Jack, a trader, is considering creating an allowance for irrecoverable debts.
State three reasons why Jack should create an allowance for irrecoverable debts. [3 marks]

....

....

....

9 Barry is a trader who makes sales on credit. During the year ending 31 December 2023, he wrote off the following debts, which he considered irrecoverable.

		$
Mar 7	Sam	170
Oct 9	Abdul	215

a Prepare the journal entry to record the write off the debt on 7 March 2023. A narrative is required. You can copy the journal below. [3 marks]

General journal			
Date	Details	Debit $	Credit $

b Prepare the irrecoverable debts account for the year ended 31 December 2023. You can copy the journal below. [3 marks]

Irrecoverable debts account					
Date	Details	$	Date	Details	$

Additional information:

- On 6 January 2024, Sam gave Barry $170 to settle his debt. Barry had no further transactions with Sam, and no other irrecoverable debts were recovered during 2024.

4 ACCOUNTING PROCEDURES

c Prepare the journal entry to record the recovery of the debt on 6 January 2024. A narrative is required. You can copy the journal below. *[5 marks]*

General journal				
Date	Details		Debit $	Credit $

d Prepare the following ledger accounts for the year ended 31 December 2024. Bring down the balances on 1 January 2025. You can copy the ledgers below. *[4 marks]*

Sam account					
Date	Details	$	Date	Details	$

Irrecoverable debts recovered from the account					
Date	Details	$	Date	Details	$

10 Murli Vadia started his trading business on 1 January 2023. He maintains an allowance for irrecoverable debts at 5 per cent of his total trade receivables. His business' financial year ends on 31 December each year.

The following balances are available for the three years ended 31 December 2023, 2024 and 2025.

	$
Trade receivables on 31 December 2023	5 000
Trade receivables on 31 December 2024	5 400
Trade receivables on 31 December 2025	4 800

a Prepare the allowance for irrecoverable debts account for each of the three years. *[7 marks]*

Allowance for irrecoverable debts account					
Date	Details	$	Date	Details	$

b Prepare relevant statement of profit or loss extracts to show changes in the allowance for irrecoverable debts for each of the three years. You can copy the statement below. *[3 marks]*

Statement of profit or loss (extracts)						
For the years ended 31 December	2023		2024		2025	
	$	$	$	$	$	$
Gross profit		xx xxx		xx xxx		xx xxx

c Prepare relevant statement of financial position extracts to show trade receivables on 31 December each year. You can copy the statement below. *[3 marks]*

Statement of financial position (extracts)						
As at 31 December	2023		2024		2025	
	$	$	$	$	$	$
Current assets						

14 Valuation of inventory

1 Ricardo bought inventory during the year ended 31 May 2024 for $15 per unit. His selling price was $25 per unit. At 31 May 2024, he had 2 000 units of inventory of which 150 units were valued at $10 each. What was the total value of inventory at 31 May 2024?

- **A** $29 250
- **B** $30 000
- **C** $42 750
- **D** $50 000 *[1 mark]*

2 Agatha provided the following information about inventory at the end of her financial year.

Product	Units held	Cost per unit	Selling and distribution costs per unit	Selling price per unit
		$	$	$
C50	100	50	3	65
AN3	250	20	3	21
B60	400	10	4	20

What is the value of her closing inventory?

- **A** $13 500
- **B** $14 000
- **C** $15 500
- **D** $19 750 *[1 mark]*

3 Sarah is a sole trader. She provided the following information about her inventory at 30 November 2025:

Product	Selling price per unit	Cost per unit	Carriage inwards
	$	$	$
X	400	340	40
Y	230	400	—
Z	170	240	—
Value of inventory recorded in statement of financial position			

4 ACCOUNTING PROCEDURES

a State the basis on which Sarah will value her inventory. *[1 mark]*

....

b Calculate the value of inventory that will be recorded in Sarah's statement of financial position at 30 November 2025. *[4 marks]*

Product	Selling price per unit	Cost per unit	Carriage inwards	Value of inventory
	$	$	$	$
X	400	340	40	
Y	230	400	—	
Z	170	240	—	
Value of inventory recorded in statement of financial position				

c State the accounting concept applied in b above. *[1 mark]*

....

4 Maximus sells tables, which he buys for $100 each. On 30 June 2025, he had five broken tables, which could only be sold for scrap at $80 each. The total cost of selling them for scrap was $75. Calculate the value of the five broken tables which should be included in Maximus' inventory at 30 June 2025. Show all your workings. *[3 marks]*

....

....

....

5 Adam runs a small business selling gardening supplies. He provided the following information about his inventory at 31 December 2025:

Item	Quantity	Purchase cost per unit	Carriage inwards per unit	Selling costs per unit	Selling price per unit
		$	$	$	$
Bags of soil	150	6.40	—	0.50	6.50
Pots	200	4.20	0.80	—	8.50
Watering cans	180	5.80	1.20	—	10.00
Packs of seeds	250	5.20	—	0.30	5.30

Calculate the value of Adam's inventory on 31 December 2025 using the table below. *[7 marks]*

	Cost per unit	Net realisable value per unit	Lower of cost and NRV		Units		Inventory valuation
Bags of soil				×		=	
Pots				×		=	
Watering cans				×		=	
Packs of seeds				×		=	
Total							

5 Preparation of financial statements

Student's Book Chapters 15–20

15 Sole traders

1. Which statement describes a statement of profit or loss?

    A A business' income and expenditure for a particular period – usually a year.

    B A list of all the assets, liabilities and owner's equity on a particular date.

    C A list of the balances of all the ledger accounts of a business on a particular date.

    D A summary of a business' receipts and payments during a particular period – usually a year. *[1 mark]*

2. How is cost of sales calculated?

    A Closing inventory + opening inventory – purchases

    B Closing inventory + purchases – opening inventory

    C Closing inventory + purchases + opening inventory

    D Opening inventory + purchases – closing inventory *[1 mark]*

3. The value of Desmond's owner's equity on 31 December 2024 is less than that on 1 January 2024. Desmond did not introduce new capital or make any drawings.

    Which term describes the difference in Desmond's owner's equity?

    A Gross loss

    B Gross profit

    C Loss for the year

    D Profit for the year *[1 mark]*

4. Which of the following operates as a trading business?

    A A builder

    B A chemist

    C A lawyer

    D A website designer *[1 mark]*

5. Djarak, a sole trader, provides the following information:

	$
Cost of sales	50 000
Expenses	4 700
Profit for the year	10 000

    What are Djarak's sales?

    A $14 700

    B $54 700

    C $60 000

    D $64 700 *[1 mark]*

6. If the owner pays the business' rent from his personal bank account, how does this affect the financial statements?

    A Increase in capital, decrease in bank balance

    B Increase in expenses, decrease in bank balance

    C Increase in expenses, increase in capital

    D Increase in expenses, increase in drawings *[1 mark]*

5 PREPARATION OF FINANCIAL STATEMENTS

7 Felcy had $56 000 in her capital account on 1 January 2025. During the year, she withdrew $4 500 cash from the business bank account and took inventory for her personal use of $1 000. Her profit for the year was $15 700. Copy the ledger below and prepare Felcy's capital account at 31 December 2025. *[6 marks]*

Felcy's capital account					
Date	Details	$	Date	Details	$

8 Identify whether the following statements are true or false by writing the word 'true' or 'false' in the following table. *[5 marks]*

		True/False
A	A service business must prepare a trading account	
B	Non-current assets are listed in the statement of financial position in the order of the length of their economic life	
C	Profit for the year decreases the owner's capital	
D	The trading and profit and loss sections make up the statement of profit or loss	
E	Carriage outwards is the cost of transporting goods to the customer	

9 Identify the missing figures by completing the following. *[5 marks]*

	Sales	Cost of sales	Gross profit/loss
	$	$	$
A	6 700	2 400	
B		3 000	1 100 (profit)
C	3 600		800 (profit)
D		4 900	300 (loss)
E	3 000		500 (loss)

10 State **two** advantages and **two** disadvantages of working as a sole trader. *[4 marks]*

Advantages:

....

....

....

....

Disadvantages:

....

....

....

....

11 State what a statement of profit or loss is and explain why it is prepared. [4 marks]

....

....

....

12 State what a statement of financial position is and explain why it is prepared. [4 marks]

....

....

....

13 Explain why gross profit is recorded in the financial statements of a trading business but not in the financial statements of a service business. [3 marks]

....

....

....

5 PREPARATION OF FINANCIAL STATEMENTS

14 Leroy is a trader with a financial year end of 31 October. The following balances were extracted from his books of account on 31 October 2025.

	$	
Sales	195 600	
Sales returns	600	
Purchases	87 150	
Carriage inwards	450	
Rent	12 000	
Wages and salaries	25 600	
Drawings	4 500	
Operating expenses	52 600	
Interest	250	
Loose tools	400	
Motor vehicles	17 000	
Fixtures and fittings	8 000	
Provision for depreciation of motor vehicles	3 400	
Provision for depreciation of fixtures and fittings	2 400	
Allowance for irrecoverable debts	260	
Inventory at 1 November 2024	22 100	
Trade receivables	14 120	
Trade payables	14 600	
Bank	780	debit
Capital at 1 November 2024	19 290	
5% bank loan repayable in 2031	10 000	

Additional information at 31 October 2025:

- The value of trade receivables included a debt of $120, which was considered unlikely to be paid.
- The allowance for irrecoverable debts was to be maintained at 2 per cent of trade receivables.
- Loose tools were valued at $320.
- Depreciation for the year on motor vehicles, fixtures and fittings was yet to be provided. Leroy depreciates his motor vehicles at the rate of 20 per cent per annum using the reducing balance method. He depreciates his fixtures and fittings at 10 per cent per annum using the straight-line method.
- During the year, Leroy took goods costing $2 000 from the business for his own use.
- Inventory at the year end was valued at $19 800.
- Accrued operating expenses at the year end amounted to $1 650. There was also some unpaid interest on the bank loan.

a Prepare the interest account for the year ended 31 October 2025. Balance the account and bring down the balance on 1 November 2025. You can copy the ledger below. [4 marks]

Interest account

Date	Details	$	Date	Details	$

b Prepare the statement of profit or loss for the year ended 31 October 2025. *[20 marks]*

Leroy			
Statement of profit or loss for the year ended 31 October 2025			
	$	$	$

Workings:

....

....

....

....

5 PREPARATION OF FINANCIAL STATEMENTS

c Prepare the statement of financial position at 31 October 2025. *[20 marks]*

Statement of financial position at 31 October 2025			
	Cost	Accumulated depreciation	Net book value
	$	$	$

Workings:

....

....

....

....

16 Partnerships

1 What will affect gross profit?
   A Carriage outwards
   B Discounts allowed
   C Discounts received
   D Goods taken by one of the partners for their personal use *[1 mark]*

2 A partnership drew up an appropriation account at the end of their financial year. Which statement is correct?

   A Interest on capital and salaries will decrease residual profit.

   B Interest on drawings and interest on loans decrease residual profit.

   C Interest on loans and salaries increase residual profit.

   D Salaries and interest on capital increase residual profit. *[1 mark]*

3 Tanesha and Delilah are in a partnership. They share profits and losses equally after Tanesha is paid a salary of $10 000. The profit for the year is $49 000. Tanesha's drawings are $11 000, and Delilah's drawings are $9 000. There is no interest on capital or drawings.

   What will Tanesha's total share of the profit be?

   A $5 000 **C** $19 500

   B $10 000 **D** $29 500 *[1 mark]*

4 Lina and Tina are in partnership, sharing profits and losses equally. Their partnership agreement states that interest is to be charged on partners' drawings.

   Which entries will be made to record the interest on drawings? *[1 mark]*

	Account(s) debited	Account(s) credited
A	Lina's and Tina's current accounts	Appropriation account
B	Lina's and Tina's current accounts	Statement of profit or loss
C	Statement of profit or loss	Lina's and Tina's current accounts
D	Appropriation account	Lina's and Tina's current accounts

5 Chang and Derek are in partnership. Which of the following will appear in their statement of profit or loss prepared at the end of the financial year?

   A Chang's salary

   B Drawings made by Chang and Derek

   C Interest on drawings made by Chang and Derek

   D Interest on loan from Derek *[1 mark]*

6 What is one key advantage of forming a partnership over a sole trader?

   A Unlimited liability

   B Increased capital investment

   C Sole decision-making

   D Better control *[1 mark]*

7 Which of the following is a disadvantage of forming a partnership?

   A Limited liability for partners

   B Losses are shared

   C Profits are shared

   D Unlimited liability for each partner *[1 mark]*

8 Rahila and Poppy are in partnership, sharing profits and losses in the ratio 1:2.

   Their partnership agreement stated the following:

   - Rahila is to be paid a salary of $10 000 per annum.
   - Interest on capital is allowed at 5 per cent per annum.
   - Interest to be charged on each partner's total drawings for the year at 5 per cent per annum.
   - The ratio is 1:2.

   The balances on the partners' capital accounts at 1 June 2024 were:

	$
Rahila	25 000
Poppy	30 000

   The partners' drawings for the year ended 31 May 2025 were:

	$
Rahila	10 000
Poppy	12 000

   The profit for the year of the partnership for the year ended 31 May 2025 was $91 000.

5 PREPARATION OF FINANCIAL STATEMENTS

a Prepare the appropriation account for the partnership for the year ended 31 May 2025. *[8 marks]*

Rahila and Poppy
Appropriation account for the year ended 31 May 2025

		$	$	$

Rahila's current account in the partnership books showed a credit balance of $15 000 at 1 June 2024.

b Calculate the balance on Rahila's current account at 31 May 2025. Show your workings. You can copy the ledger below. *[7 marks]*

Rahila's current account

Date	Details	Rahila	Date	Details	Rahila
		$			$

Workings:

....

....

....

....

9 Smith and Jamil are in partnership, sharing profits and losses equally. Their gross profit for the year ended 31 August 2024 was $25 000. They provide the following information:

At 1 September 2023:

	$	
Current account balances:		
Smith	800	credit
Jamil	100	debit
Capital account balances:		
Smith	30 000	
Jamil	20 000	

For the year ended 31 August 2024:

	$
Operating expenses	10 500
Interest on capital:	
Smith	3 000
Jamil	2 000
Drawings:	
Smith	2 400
Jamil	1 500

a Calculate the partnership profit for the year ended 31 August 2024. Show your workings. *[2 marks]*

....

....

b Calculate each partner's share of the residual profit or loss for the year ended 31 August 2024. Show your workings. You can copy the account below. *[5 marks]*

		$	$

c Prepare the partners' current accounts for the year ended 31 August 2024. You can copy the ledger below. *[7 marks]*

Current accounts

Date	Details	Smith $	Jamil $	Date	Details	Smith $	Jamil $

5 PREPARATION OF FINANCIAL STATEMENTS

d Prepare an extract of the statement of financial position at 31 August 2024 showing the partner's capital and current accounts. *[5 marks]*

Smith and Jamil Statement of financial position at 31 August 2024 (extract)			
	$	$	$

10 State five reasons a sole trader might decide to form a partnership to expand the business. *[5 marks]*

....

....

....

....

....

....

....

....

11 State three disadvantages of a partnership. *[3 marks]*

....

....

....

12 a State why a partnership agreement is prepared when a partnership is formed. *[1 mark]*

....

b State three items which may be included in a partnership agreement. *[3 marks]*

....

....

....

13 Explain the purpose of an appropriation account. *[2 marks]*

....

....

14 A partnership maintains both capital and current accounts.

State whether each statement refers to a capital or a current account by entering the word 'capital' or 'current' against each statement. *[5 marks]*

	Capital/Current
It shows whether a partner has withdrawn more than he has earned	
It records the initial capital contribution of a partner	
It records drawings	
It has a balance, which usually changes every year	
It records interest on capital	

17 Limited companies

1 A limited company has an issued share capital of 100 000 ordinary shares of $1 each.

Retained earnings at 1 January 2024 were $15 000. An interim dividend of $0.10 per ordinary share was paid during the year.

Profit for the year ended 31 December 2024 was $50 000. A transfer of $10 000 was made to the general reserve.

What was the balance on the retained earnings account on 31 December 2024?

- A $45 000
- B $50 000
- C $60 000
- D $65 000 *[1 mark]*

2 Which item does **not** appear in the statement of changes in equity of a company?

- A Debenture interest
- B Interim dividend paid
- C Retained earnings at the start of the year
- D Transfer to general reserve *[1 mark]*

3 A limited company has 200 000 ordinary shares of $1 each. An interim dividend of $0.02 per share was paid during the year. The directors proposed a final dividend of $0.10 per share.

What is the total amount of ordinary dividends shown in the statement of changes in equity for the year?

- A $4 000
- B $20 000
- C $24 000
- D $40 000 *[1 mark]*

4 A company is financed by:
- 20 000 ordinary shares of $0.50 each.
- $4 000 10 per cent loan.

Profit for the year before interest is $3 000.

What is the maximum dividend payable per share from this year's profits?

- A $0.13
- B $0.15
- C $0.18
- D $0.30 *[1 mark]*

5 A company provides the following information for the year ended 31 December 2024:

	$
Total assets	525 750
Total liabilities	200 000

5 PREPARATION OF FINANCIAL STATEMENTS

What was the company's total equity on 31 December 2024?

- A $200 000
- B $325 750
- C $525 750
- D $725 750

[1 mark]

6 Which statement describes the principle of limited liability in a limited company?

- A Shareholders are exempt from all business liabilities
- B Shareholders are personally liable for company debts
- C Shareholders can lose only the amount they invested
- D Shareholders have unlimited financial exposure

[1 mark]

7 Define the following terms:

a Dividend [1 mark]

....

....

b Debentures [1 mark]

....

....

c Total equity [1 mark]

....

....

d Called-up capital [1 mark]

....

....

e Issued capital [1 mark]

....

....

8 Explain two features of:

a Ordinary shares [4 marks]

....

....

....

b Debentures [4 marks]

....

....

....

9 Josh Limited provided the following information at 1 June 2024:
- Ordinary share capital comprises 200 000 ordinary shares of $0.50 each.
- General reserves $100 000.
- The balance on the retained earnings account was $18 000.
- The company has 5 per cent debentures, $50 000.
- Profit for the year ended 31 May 2025 was $7 000.

Prepare an extract from the statement of financial position of Josh Limited at 31 May 2025 to show the issued share capital and reserves. *[3 marks]*

Josh Limited Statement of financial position at 31 May 2025 (extract)	
	$
Equity and liabilities:	
Equity:	

10 On 1 January 2024, Gilchrest Limited's statement of financial position included the following:

	$
Ordinary share capital ($1 share)	50 000
General reserve	15 000
Retained earnings	5 000

During the year ended 31 December 2024, Gilchrest Limited:
- Issued 50 000 additional ordinary shares of $1 each
- Paid a final dividend of $2 000 from the year ended 31 December 2023
- Paid an interim dividend of $0.10 per share on all shares held at the beginning of the year
- Made a profit for the year of $60 000.

At 31 December 2024, the directors:
- Transferred $10 000 to the general reserve
- Proposed a final dividend of $0.20 per share.

5 PREPARATION OF FINANCIAL STATEMENTS

a Prepare the statement of changes in equity for Gilchrest Limited for the year ended 31 December 2024. *[9 marks]*

Gilchrest Limited Statement of changes in equity for the year ended 31 December 2024				
	Share capital	General reserve	Retained earnings	Total
	$	$	$	$

b Prepare the equity section of the statement of financial position at 31 December 2024. *[4 marks]*

Equity	$

11 Enrique has been a sole trader for some years. He is now considering changing his business structure.

Advise Enrique whether he should turn his business into a limited company. Justify your answer. *[5 marks]*

....

....

....

....

....

....

12 State what is meant by the term 'limited liability'. *[1 mark]*

....

....

13 Vikram is a window cleaner who cleaned the windows of a big office building belonging to a limited company. He is concerned that the company might leave the business before paying him for his work.

Discuss whether Vikram's situation would be better if a partnership owned the office building. [4 marks]

....

....

....

....

14 a Explain **two** advantages of operating as a limited company compared to other business structures such as sole trader or partnership. [4 marks]

....

....

....

....

b State **two** disadvantages of operating as a limited company compared to other business structures such as sole trader or partnership. [2 marks]

....

....

....

....

18 Clubs and societies

1 Which term describes the balancing figure in a receipts and payments account?

    A Excess of expenditure over income

    B Profit from trading activity

    C Surplus of income over expenditure

    D Year-end cash and bank balances [1 mark]

2 The following information relates to sports equipment owned by the Hurray Sports Club for the year ended 31 August 2025.

2024		$
Sep 01	Book value of sports equipment	5 000
Oct 31	Equipment purchased	1 100
2025		
Jan 02	Repairs to equipment	60
Aug 31	Depreciation of equipment	330

5 PREPARATION OF FINANCIAL STATEMENTS

What amount will be shown as the charge for sports equipment in the income and expenditure account for the year ended 31 August 2025?

A $60

B $330

C $390

D $5 330

[1 mark]

3 The Jolly Cricket Club has 100 members. Some members had not paid their subscriptions for the year ended 31 July 2025. No adjustment has been made for unpaid subscriptions in the club's income and expenditure account for the year ended 31 July 2025.

What is the effect of this error? [1 mark]

	Surplus of income over expenditure	Statement of financial position
A	Overstated	Current assets overstated
B	Overstated	Current liabilities overstated
C	Understated	Current assets understated
D	Understated	Current liabilities understated

4 a State what is meant by the term 'subscription' in a club's accounting records. *[1 mark]*

....

....

b Explain why a subscription account can have both a debit and a credit opening balance. *[2 marks]*

....

....

....

c The Torbay Activity Club's members pay an annual subscription of $250 each.

The following information is available for the year ended 31 October 2025:

- On 1 November 2024, eight members paid their subscriptions in advance for the financial year ending 31 October 2025.
- During the year ended 31 October 2025, 150 members paid their annual subscription in full.
- On 31 October 2025, subscriptions due from ten members remained unpaid.

18 Clubs and societies

Prepare the subscriptions account in the books of the Torbay Activity Club for the year ended 31 October 2025. Balance the account on 31 October 2025 and bring down the balance on 1 November 2025. Show the amount transferred to the income and expenditure account. You can copy the ledger below. *[5 marks]*

	The Torbay Activity Club Subscriptions account				
Date	Details	$	Date	Details	$

5 The term used in the financial statements of a sole trader is given in the first column of the following table. Complete the table by writing in the second column the equivalent term in the financial statements of a club or society. The first one has been completed as an example. *[4 marks]*

Sole trader	Club or society
Loss for the year	Deficit (excess of expenditure over income)
Statement of profit or loss	
Owner's equity	
Profit for the year	
Cash book	

6 Complete the following table by placing a tick (✓) in each row to indicate whether the item would appear in the income and expenditure account or the receipts and payments account.

The first one has been completed as an example. *[5 marks]*

	Income and expenditure account	Receipts and payments account
Profit from competition	✓	
Profit from the sale of furniture		
Purchase of furniture by bank transfer		
Proceeds from the sale of furniture		
Subscriptions owing written off		
Depreciation of furniture		

7 Plucky Recreation Club provided the following information:

	$
Payment made to suppliers of café inventory for the year ended 31 August 2025	3 500
Owing to suppliers of café inventory at 31 August 2024	150
Owing to suppliers of café inventory at 31 August 2025	180

5 PREPARATION OF FINANCIAL STATEMENTS

a Copy and complete the trading account for the Plucky Recreation Club for the year ended 31 August 2025.

[4 marks]

Plucky Recreation Club
Trading account for the year ended 31 August 2025

	$	$
Revenue		8 500
Inventory – 1 September 2024	410	
Purchases	....	
	....	
Inventory – 31 August 2025	....	
Cost of sales		....
Gross profit		6 500

At 1 September 2024, the club balance on the accumulated fund was $15 560. At that date, $20 was outstanding for travelling expenses, and insurance was prepaid by $50.

The treasurer provided the following information from the receipts and payments account relating to the year ended 31 August 2025:

	$
Subscriptions received	2 400
Payment of fees	40
Rent received	350
Travelling expenses	400
Sundry expenses	2 300
Insurance	320
Receipts from spectators	2 000
Proceeds from fundraiser	500

Additional information:

- At 31 August 2025, insurance prepaid amounted to $30, and subscriptions owing amounted to $140.
- Equipment is to be depreciated by $500.

b Prepare the income and expenditure account for the year ended 31 August 2025. *[5 marks]*

Plucky Recreation Club		
Income and expenditure account for the year ended 31 August 2025		
	$	$

c Prepare an extract of the statement of financial position showing the accumulated fund for the year ended 31 August 2025. *[2 marks]*

Plucky Recreation Club		
Statement of financial position at 31 August 2025 (extract)		
	$	$
Accumulated fund:		

8 Explain why there are no drawings in a club or society. *[2 marks]*

....

....

9 Gavaskar Cricket Club has had a deficit for the last two years. As a result, they do not have the funds to repair and maintain the facilities at the club. The treasurer thinks the club will have another deficit this year as well.

Suggest four ways that could be used to improve the situation. *[4 marks]*

....

....

....

....

5 PREPARATION OF FINANCIAL STATEMENTS

10 Compare the term 'capital' used in a business and 'accumulated fund' used in club accounts. *[4 marks]*

....

....

....

....

....

19 Manufacturing accounts

1 How is the factory cost of production calculated?

  A Factory overheads + prime cost − increase in work in progress

  B Factory overheads + prime cost + increase in work in progress

  C Prime cost − factory overheads − increase in work in progress

  D Prime cost + increase in work in progress − factory overheads   *[1 mark]*

2 Saleem, a manufacturer, provided the following information.

	$
Direct labour	3 500
Direct materials	5 400
Factory overheads	10 000

  What is the prime cost?

  A $8 900   **C** $15 400

  B $13 500   **D** $18 900   *[1 mark]*

3 Which of these is a factory overhead?

  A Carriage on finished goods

  B Cost of raw materials

  C Direct labour

  D Factory supervisor's salary   *[1 mark]*

4 Which of these is a direct production cost?

  A Carriage outwards

  B Factory rent

  C Factory supervisor's salary

  D Machine operator wages   *[1 mark]*

5 The following items relate to a manufacturing business which sometimes purchases goods in finished form to meet their customers' demands.

  i) Carriage inwards

  ii) Carriage outwards

  iii) Purchases of material

  iv) Purchases of finished goods

  Which items will be included in the manufacturing account?

  A i) and iii)

  B i), ii) and iii)

  C i), iii) and iv)

  D i), ii), iii) and iv)   *[1 mark]*

6 Explain the difference between:

  a A trader and a manufacturer   *[2 marks]*

....

....

b Direct and indirect costs [2 marks]

....

....

7 Tom Li is a manufacturer. He provides the following information.

	$
Inventory at 1 July 2024	
Raw materials	12 000
Work in progress	3 500
Finished goods	6 700
For the year ended 30 June 2025	
Purchases of raw materials	55 000
Revenue	360 000
Carriage inwards	3 700
Factory wages:	
Direct	16 000
Indirect	10 000
Factory fuel and power	8 000
Factory rent	15 000
Depreciation on factory machinery	4 000
Inventory at 30 June 2025	
Raw materials	10 000
Work in progress	3 900
Finished goods	4 500

Additional information:
- Inventory at 30 June 2025 was: raw materials $10 000; finished goods $4 500.
- There was no work in progress at the beginning or end of the year.
- Depreciation $4 000 is to be charged on factory machinery for the year ended 30 June 2025.

5 PREPARATION OF FINANCIAL STATEMENTS

a Prepare Tom Li's manufacturing account for the year ended 30 June 2025.
Show prime cost and cost of production. *[5 marks]*

Tom Li Manufacturing account for the year ended 30 June 2025		
	$	$

b Prepare Tom Li's trading account for the year ended 30 June 2025. *[4 marks]*

Tom Li Trading account for the year ended 30 June 2025		
	$	$

8 State three types of inventory that a manufacturing business can hold. *[3 marks]*

....

20 Incomplete records

1 Hugh provided the following information:

	$
Owner's equity at 31 December 2025	38 000
Profit for the year	7 000
Owner's equity introduced during the year	2 500

What was Hugh's owner's equity at 1 January 2025?

- **A** $21 000
- **B** $29 000
- **C** $34 500
- **D** $42 500 *[1 mark]*

2 Belinda does not keep a complete set of accounting records.

Which information is needed to calculate her total net sales?

- **A** Cash discount received
- **B** Inventory returned by customers
- **C** Inventory returned to suppliers
- **D** Trade discount allowed *[1 mark]*

3 Aleena is a sole trader. She does not keep a complete set of accounting records.

How is her profit for the year calculated?

- **A** Closing capital – opening capital + capital introduced
- **B** Closing capital – opening capital – capital introduced + drawings
- **C** Closing capital – opening capital + capital introduced – drawings
- **D** Closing capital – opening capital – drawings *[1 mark]*

4 Tatyana produced a statement of affairs at 31 December 2023 and 31 December 2024.

- Depreciation for the year was $300.
- During 2024, her long-term loan increased by $2 500, and her net current assets decreased by $1 500.

By how much did the total of Tatyana's owner's equity decrease?

- **A** $1 500
- **B** $2 500
- **C** $4 000
- **D** $4 300 *[1 mark]*

5 Simran is a sole trader. Her owner's equity is lower at 31 December 2025 than at 31 December 2024. She had not contributed any additional capital to the business.

What does this mean?

- **A** Simran's business has made a loss.
- **B** Simran's business has made a profit.
- **C** Simran has taken a long-term business loan.
- **D** Simran sold some non-current assets during the year ended 31 December 2025. *[1 mark]*

6 In which scenarios might a business choose a single-entry or cash-based system over a complete double-entry system?

- **A** When the business has complex financial transactions
- **B** When the business has minimal transactions and wants to reduce costs
- **C** When the business needs to meet strict regulatory requirements
- **D** When the business operates in multiple countries

7 Bella, a sole trader, does not keep a complete set of double-entry accounts.

State **two** advantages to Bella of maintaining a complete set of double-entry accounts. *[2 marks]*

....

....

....

....

5 PREPARATION OF FINANCIAL STATEMENTS

8 State **two** reasons why a small business might not maintain a complete double-entry accounting system. *[2 marks]*

....

....

9 Kiran, a sole trader, provided the following information:

	1 June 2024	31 May 2025
	$	$
Non-current assets at cost	20 000	30 000
Accumulated depreciation	8 000	?
Current assets	10 000	12 000
Non-current liabilities	1 500	2 500

- Kiran depreciates her non-current assets at 10 per cent per annum using the straight-line method of depreciation.
- Kiran took drawings of $7 500 during the year.

a Calculate the accumulated depreciation on non-current assets at 31 May 2025. *[2 marks]*

....

....

....

b Prepare a statement of affairs for Kiran at 1 June 2024 and 31 May 2025. *[10 marks]*

Kiran Statement of affairs at 1 June 2024	
	$

Kiran
Statement of affairs at 31 May 2025

	$

c Calculate Kiran's profit or loss for the year ended 31 May 2025. *[3 marks]*

....

....

10 Conserva is a trader who sells only one product. In each of the five years below, she buys goods for $4 per unit and sells them at $10 per unit.

- Year 1: Conserva's opening inventory is valued at $540, and her closing inventory is $620. Her purchases for the year amount to $7 100.

a Calculate the value of her sales. *[3 marks]*

....

....

- Year 2: Conserva made sales amounting to $19 200.

b Calculate the gross profit for the year. *[2 marks]*

....

- Year 3: Trade payables at the start of the year were $692, and at the end were $704. During the year, Conserva returned 10 faulty units. She paid her credit suppliers $6 770 after deducting a $30 cash discount.

c Prepare the total trade payables account for the year to show the value of purchases. *[6 marks]*

Total trade payables account

	$		$

5 PREPARATION OF FINANCIAL STATEMENTS

- Year 4: Trade receivables at the start of the year were $1 620. Sales for the year amounted to $20 000. An irrecoverable debt of $130 was written off, and receipts from credit customers amounted to $19 910.

d Calculate the value of trade receivables at the end of the year. *[4 marks]*

....

- Year 5: Conserva thinks some goods are being stolen from her shop. Her opening inventory was $492, and her closing inventory was $388. Purchases for the year amounted to $6 920, and purchases returned to $60. Sales for the year amounted to $17 000.

e Calculate the value of the goods which were stolen:

  i) at selling price *[5 marks]*

....

....

....

  ii) at cost price. *[2 marks]*

....

11 Zahra started her business on 1 January 2024. She paid $6 000 of her personal cash into the business bank account on that date.

Zahra made all her sales and purchases on a credit basis but did not maintain proper accounting records. She kept copies of sales invoices marked as paid when funds were received. She kept all her purchase invoices and noted when she paid them.

Zahra was able to provide the following information for the year ended 31 December 2024:

- Sales invoices totalled $96 400. Of these, $14 110 were unpaid at the year's end. One debt, $200, was considered irrecoverable. Most funds received came as cheques or credit transfers, but $8 100 was received in cash.

- Purchases invoices totalled $52 600. No payments to credit suppliers had been made in cash.

- An analysis of the bank statements showed that the following payments had been made:

	$
Payments to credit suppliers	43 260
Rent	6 000
Wages	3 220
Purchases of fixtures and fittings	9 000
Operating expenses	9 100

- Zahra took drawings in cash of $550 a month throughout the year. She also paid a total of $770 for operating expenses in cash.

- Fixtures and fittings were to be depreciated at 10 per cent per annum on the straight-line basis.

- Accrued operating expenses at the year-end amounted to $110, and prepaid operating expenses amounted to $70.

- Closing inventory was valued at $1 200.

20 Incomplete records

a Prepare the total trade receivables account for the year to show the amount received from credit customers through the bank. *[5 marks]*

Total trade receivables account			
	$		$

b Prepare the statement of profit or loss for the year ended 31 December 2024. *[12 marks]*

Zahra		
Statement of profit or loss for the year ended 31 December 2024		
	$	$

Workings:

....

....

....

....

5 PREPARATION OF FINANCIAL STATEMENTS

c Prepare the statement of financial position at 31 December 2024. *[17 marks]*

Statement of financial position at 31 December 2024			
	Cost	Accumulated depreciation	Net book value
	$	$	$

Workings:

....

....

....

....

20 Incomplete records

12 At 1 April 2024, Anodiwa's business assets were as follows:
- Equipment valued at $6 000 (cost $9 000)
- Furniture $2 000
- Inventory $900
- Trade receivables $250
- Cash $300

Her trade payables totalled $1 400.

At 31 March 2025, her assets were:
- Shop, which had cost $30 000, with a loan of $25 000 still outstanding
- Equipment valued at $5 000
- Furniture $2 400
- Inventory $1 300
- Trade receivables of $300 (of which $90 were known to be irrecoverable)
- Cash $600

Her trade payables amounted to $1 000. During the year, Anodiwa's drawings amounted to $6 000, and Anodiwa also invested a further $4 000 into the business bank account.

Calculate Anodiwa's profit for the year ended 31 March 2025. *[7 marks]*

Anodiwa's profit for the year ended 31 March 2025	
	$

6 Analysis and interpretation

Student's Book Chapters 21–24

21 Calculation and understanding of accounting ratios

1. A business provides the following information:

	$
Gross profit for the year	30 000
Sales revenue for the year	80 000
Sales returns for the year	5 000

   What is the gross profit margin?

   A 30% C 37.5%
   B 31.25% D 40% *[1 mark]*

2. A business provides the following information:

	$
Gross profit	30 000
Profit for the year	20 000
Sales for the year	100 000

   What are the expenses as a percentage of sales?

   A 10% C 30%
   B 20% D 50% *[1 mark]*

3. A business provided the following information:

	$
Bank overdraft	1 100
Machinery	23 000
Inventory	4 100
Trade receivables	2 700
Cash	200
Trade payables	2 400

   What is the current ratio?

   A 0.65:1 C 2.92:1
   B 2:1 D 8.57:1 *[1 mark]*

4. Baldeep, a sole trader, sets his selling price by adding a profit figure to the cost price.

   How does he do this?

   A By applying a margin
   B By applying a mark-up
   C By applying the ROCE
   D By using the acid test (liquid) ratio *[1 mark]*

5. Chen, a sole trader, provided the following information for the year ended 31 December 2019:

	$
Inventory at 1 January	2 000
Inventory at 31 December	4 500
Cost of sales	6 000

   What are the purchases?

   A $1 500
   B $6 000
   C $7 500
   D $8 500 *[1 mark]*

6. Which of the following factors is not considered when using mark-up to determine sale prices?

   A Competitors' prices
   B Overhead costs
   C The cost price of the product
   D The number of products in inventory *[1 mark]*

7. Suggest:

   a Two drawbacks to a business of not paying trade payables on time. *[2 marks]*

   ....

   ....

b Two ways a business can improve its period of trade receivables turnover. [2 marks]

....

....

c Two reasons why a low inventory turnover rate is unsuitable for a business. [2 marks]

....

....

d One reason why it is important for a business to know its acid test (liquid) ratio. [1 mark]

....

e Two ways a business can improve its current ratio. [2 marks]

....

....

8 Define the following terms:
   a Capital employed [2 marks]

....

....

   b Working capital [2 marks]

....

....

   c Return on capital employed [2 marks]

....

....

   d Rate of inventory turnover [2 marks]

....

....

9 Explain **two** disadvantages to a business of having insufficient working capital. [4 marks]

....

....

6 ANALYSIS AND INTERPRETATION

10 Alain Traders provides the following information:

	$	$
Capital:		
Opening	22 000	
Add: Profit for the year	3 450	
	25 450	
Less: Drawings	1 650	23 800
Non-current liabilities:		
Loan from bank		10 000
Current liabilities:		
Creditors		5 000
Total capital and liabilities		38 800

Interest paid on the bank loan during the year was $600.

Calculate Alain Traders' ROCE. Show your answer correct to two decimal places. *[3 marks]*

11 Didi provides the following information:

	$	$
Non-current assets		45 000
Current assets:		
Inventory	4 000	
Trade receivables	3 600	
Other receivables	400	
Cash and cash equivalents	1 000	9 000
Total assets		54 000
Additional information:		
Sales revenue		100 000 (includes $64 000 cash sales)
Credit purchases		60 000
Trade payables		5 900
Opening inventory		6 000

The rate of inventory was 13 times.

a Calculate the trade receivables turnover in days. *[2 marks]*

b Calculate the trade payables turnover in days. [2 marks]

....

....

....

....

c Calculate the cost of sales. [3 marks]

....

....

....

....

12 a Explain what inventory turnover (in days) measures. [2 marks]

....

....

b Why is inventory turnover (in days) an important ratio for a business? [2 marks]

....

....

c Discuss whether a business should have a higher or lower inventory turnover (in days). [2 marks]

....

....

....

....

22 Interpretation of accounting ratios and inter-business comparisons

1 The acid test (liquid) ratio of Gracie's business was 1.5:1 in 2024 and 0.6:1 in 2025.

What does a comparison of these ratios show?

A Gracie controlled her expenses better in 2024

B Gracie's business is more liquid in 2024

C Gracie's gross profit is better in 2024

D Grace's profit for the year is better in 2025. [1 mark]

2 The table shows the performance of Moussa's businesses in 2024 and 2025:

	2024	2025
Gross margin	33%	25%
Profit margin	10%	11.2%

6 ANALYSIS AND INTERPRETATION

What is revealed by comparing the ratios?

A Moussa controls his expenses better in 2024.

B Moussa controls his expenses better in 2025.

C Moussa's cost of sales is higher in 2024.

D Moussa's cost of sales is higher in 2025. *[1 mark]*

3 A bakery business has calculated the following ratios.

	Year ended 30 June 2024	Year ended 30 June 2025
Gross margin	30%	35%

Why did the bakery's gross profit margin increase in the year ended 30 June 2025?

A The bakery's cost of sales increased

B The bakery's expenses decreased

C The bakery's expenses increased

D The bakery's selling price increased *[1 mark]*

4 Imran and Ali make the following business forecasts for the next financial year.

	Imran	Ali
Average inventory at cost	$90 000	$80 000
Rate of inventory turnover	5 times	6 times
Mark-up	20%	25%

Who is forecasting more sales for the next financial year?

A Ali at $120 000

B Ali at $600 000

C Imran at $90 000

D Imran at $540 000 *[1 mark]*

5 Faye and Kaye own similar businesses. The following information is provided.

	Faye	Kaye
	$	$
Sales revenue	100 000	80 000
Expenses	30 000	25 000
Profit for the year	40 000	35 000

Which of the following statements is true?

A Faye's gross profit margin of 40% is better than Kaye's 35%.

B Faye's gross profit margin of 70% is better than Kaye's 60%.

C Kaye's gross profit margin of 70% is better than Faye's 75%.

D Kaye's gross profit margin of 75% is better than Faye's 70%. *[1 mark]*

6 Two companies are using ratio analysis to interpret their financial statements. Which ratio is calculated using information from the statement of financial position and the statement of profit or loss?

A Gross profit margin

B Profit margin

C ROCE

D Working capital ratio *[1 mark]*

7 Why might a business have a cash surplus but a low profit?

A Because of high credit sales.

B Because of significant non-cash expenses.

C Because it has good control over its expenses.

D Because of lower depreciation expenses. *[1 mark]*

8 Suggest three ways in which ratios can be used.

[3 marks]

....

....

....

....

9 Kareena is a trader. Her financial year ends on 31 December. She provided the following summary of her assets and liabilities on 31 December 2025:

	$	$
Non-current assets		170 500
Inventory		20 400
Trade receivables		38 000
Cash in hand		5 100
		234 000
Capital at 1 January 2025	100 000	
Profit for the year	62 000	162 000
Trade payables		30 600
Bank overdraft		11 400
Long-term loan		30 000
		234 000

Kareena also provided information from her statement of profit or loss:

	$
Sales revenue	500 000
Cost of sales	340 000
Expenses	98 000

Kareena wishes to compare her business performance for the year ended 31 December 2025 with that of the previous financial year.

a Complete the following table to show the ratios for Kareena's business for the year ended 31 December 2025. Calculations should be correct to two decimal places. *[4 marks]*

Ratio	Year ended 31 December	
	2024	2025
Gross margin	25%	32%
Profit margin	11%	12.40%
Current ratio	2.5:1	1.51:1
Acid test (liquid) ratio	0.9:1	1.03:1

b Compare the ratios for 2024 with those of 2025:

i) Gross profit margin *[1 mark]*

....

....

ii) Profit margin *[1 mark]*

....

....

iii) Current ratio *[1 mark]*

....

....

6 ANALYSIS AND INTERPRETATION

iv) Acid test (liquid) ratio *[1 mark]*

....

....

c Compare Kareena's profitability in the year ended 31 December 2025 with the year ended 31 December 2024. *[2 marks]*

....

....

....

d Suggest **two** reasons for the change in the gross profit margin. *[2 marks]*

....

....

e State the year in which Kareena had better control over her expenses. Give a reason for your answer.

Year ended 31 December *[1 mark]*

Reason: *[1 mark]*

....

....

....

....

f Complete the following table by placing a tick (✓) in the correct column to show how each transaction would affect the current ratio. *[3 marks]*

	Decrease	Increase	No effect
Kareena took inventory for her personal use			
Kareena purchased some furniture on credit			
Kareen received a long-term loan			

g State whether Kareena would be satisfied with the change in her liquidity position. Give a reason for your answer.

Satisfied? *[1 mark]*

....

Reason: *[1 mark]*

....

....

....

....

10 Hassan is a sole trader and provides the following information for the year ended 31 December 2025:

	$
Inventory at 1 January 2025	12 000
Inventory at 31 December 2025	10 000
Purchases	200 000
Sales	250 000

   a Calculate Hassan's rate of inventory turnover for the year ended 31 December 2025. Your calculation should be correct to two decimal places. *[3 marks]*

   b Calculate Hassan's gross profit margin for the year ended 31 December 2025. Your calculation should be correct to two decimal places. *[3 marks]*

The industry figures were as follows:

Rate of inventory turnover	12 times
Gross margin	18%

   c State whether Hassan's ratios are better or worse than the industry figures:

      i) Rate of inventory turnover *[1 mark]*

      ii) Gross profit margin *[1 mark]*

   d Suggest one reason for the difference between the industry figures and Hassan's.

      i) Rate of inventory turnover *[1 mark]*

      ii) Gross profit margin *[1 mark]*

11 Identify **two** factors a sole trader should consider when comparing results with those of another business. *[2 marks]*

6 ANALYSIS AND INTERPRETATION

12 a Explain the acid test (liquid) ratio. *[2 marks]*

....

....

b Suggest how the short-term financial health of a business can be affected by an acid test (liquid) ratio:

i) above 1:1

....

....

ii) below 1:1. *[4 marks]*

....

....

13 A company reports the following changes:
- 15 per cent increase in gross profit from $550 000
- 6 per cent decrease in other incomes from $110 000
- 20 per cent increase in expenses from $350 000.

Calculate the overall percentage change in the profit for the year. *[4 marks]*

....

....

....

....

....

....

23 Interested parties

1 Which of the following is an internal user of accounting information?

A Customers

B Owners of the business

C The bank

D The government *[1 mark]*

2 Which of the following is **not** an internal user of accounting information?

A Managers

B Owners

C Partners

D The government *[1 mark]*

23 Interested parties

3 What do suppliers look for while analysing a business' financial statements?

  A Customer satisfaction
  B Employee turnover
  C Environmental impact of operations
  D Short-term liquidity position [1 mark]

4 The following information was extracted from the financial statements of a sole trader:

	$
Profit for the year	7 000
Capital employed	56 000
Sales	50 000

  a Identify two users of accounting information who would be interested in the information above. Give reasons for your answer. [4 marks]

  ....

  ....

  b State which accounting ratios would assist those users identified in part a in analysing the information. [2 marks]

  ....

  ....

5 State one reason why each of the following interested parties might wish to look at the financial statements of a business:

  a Tax authorities [1 mark]

  ....

  ....

  b Employees [1 mark]

  ....

  ....

  c Suppliers [1 mark]

  ....

  ....

  d Club members [1 mark]

  ....

  ....

6 ANALYSIS AND INTERPRETATION

e The general public [1 mark]

....

....

6 Explain how employees can use accounting information to assess job security and promotion opportunities. [4 marks]

....

....

....

....

....

....

24 Limitations of accounting statements

1 Which group contains an intangible asset?

  A Cash and cash equivalents, inventory, trade receivables

  B Customer satisfaction, motor vehicle, furniture

  C Fixtures, stationery, machinery

  D Sales, cost of sales, expenses [1 mark]

2 Which of these is **not** a limitation of financial statements?

  A Different definitions used globally

  B Financial aspects

  C Historic cost

  D Non-financial aspects [1 mark]

3 Historic cost is the value of an asset based on:

  A its market value

  B its realisable value

  C what the business thinks it is worth

  D what was paid at the time of purchase [1 mark]

4 Which of the following is **not** a primary area covered by accounting policies?

  A Marketing strategy

  B Revenue recognition

  C Treatment of expenses

  D Valuation of assets [1 mark]

5 What is the effect of using different depreciation methods for asset valuation in financial statements?

  A Consistent asset values across all companies

  B Different reported values for the same type of asset

24 Limitations of accounting statements

    C Increase in revenue

    D No impact on the financial statements   *[1 mark]*

6 Explain **three** limitations of financial statements.   *[6 marks]*

....

....

....

....

....

....

7 Explain how different revenue recognition policies affect the comparability of financial statements between companies.   *[4 marks]*

....

....

....

....

8 Complete the following table by indicating with a tick (✓) whether the information can be measured in quantitative terms.   *[5 marks]*

Information	✓
The business has suppliers that deliver quality goods on time	
Improved public roads to the business property	
The business owns property in the centre of the city	
Increase in efficiency following staff training	
The business owns a motor vehicle	

9 Explain how non-financial factors such as brand reputation, employee satisfaction and environmental sustainability impact a company's performance beyond what is shown in the accounting statements.   *[4 marks]*

....

....

....

....

....

....

7 Accounting concepts and modern practices

Student's Book Chapters 25–27

25 Accounting concepts

1. Which statement refers to the going concern concept?

   A Accounting records are prepared assuming that the business will continue to operate in the near future.

   B A non-current asset should be recorded at its original cost in the statement of financial position.

   C Income and expenses should be accounted for the same way every year.

   D Profits are calculated after accruals and prepayments are accounted for. *[1 mark]*

2. A salary payment was entered in the cash book, and the salary account in the general ledger.

   Which accounting concept was applied?

   A Duality   C Materiality

   B Matching   D Prudence *[1 mark]*

3. What is the meaning of the money measurement concept?

   A Non-current assets usually are shown at cost price.

   B Only items with a monetary value are included in the accounts.

   C Profits are calculated based on cash received less cash paid.

   D Profit should not be anticipated, and losses should be written off as soon as they are known. *[1 mark]*

4. Malcolm, a sole trader, decided that office equipment costing less than $300 would not be regarded as a non-current asset.

   Which accounting concept is being applied?

   A Duality   C Materiality

   B Matching   D Money measurement *[1 mark]*

5. What is ensured by applying the concept of consistency?

   A Business' assets are recorded at cost price.

   B Financial statements should be drawn up using the same methods from year to year.

   C Results of a business can be compared with those of similar businesses.

   D The statement of financial position excludes items which have no monetary value. *[1 mark]*

6. Alessandro thinks his business will be worth more when he employs new, highly skilled staff.

   Which accounting concept prevents him from recording this in his statement of financial position?

   A Business entity C Historic cost

   B Duality   D Money measurement *[1 mark]*

7. What is the main difference between the matching and accrual concepts?

   A The matching concept aligns expenses with the revenues they help to generate, while the accrual concept involves recognising expenses and income when they are paid or received.

   B The matching concept aligns expenses with related revenues, while the accrual concept recognises expenses and revenues when they are incurred or earned.

25 Accounting concepts

C The matching concept involves recognising expenses when paid, while the accrual concept recognises expenses when incurred.

D The matching concept is cash-based, while the accrual concept is not. *[1 mark]*

8 Selma applies the historical cost concept and records all her non-current assets at the actual cost.

State one advantage of applying this concept. *[1 mark]*

....

9 A multinational company has prepared financial statements without including very small items of fixtures in its non-current assets.

Identify the accounting concept applied by the company. *[1 mark]*

....

10 Amelia provides the following information about her financial statements:

Event	Recorded/Not recorded
Better staff morale following redecoration of property	Not recorded in financial statements
Installation of air conditioning to improve staff comfort	Recorded in financial statements

State which concept is being followed by Amelia. *[1 mark]*

....

11 Assets and liabilities are recorded in the financial statements at the actual amount of the transaction.

Identify the accounting concept which is being applied. *[1 mark]*

....

12 Define the following accounting concepts:

a Matching *[1 mark]*

....

....

b Prudence *[1 mark]*

....

....

c Realisation *[1 mark]*

....

....

13 a Explain the accrual concept in accounting. *[2 marks]*

....

....

7 ACCOUNTING CONCEPTS AND MODERN PRACTICES

b Compare accrual accounting with cash-based accounting. *[2 marks]*

....

....

....

26 Ethical considerations

1 Professional competence requires accountants to:
   - **A** have adequate knowledge about their job
   - **B** keep the financial details of their clients to themselves
   - **C** provide accurate financial data to stakeholders
   - **D** use their skills and expertise responsibly *[1 mark]*

2 Which of the following is **not** included in the fundamental ethical principles developed by accounting bodies?
   - **A** Confidentiality
   - **B** Subjectivity
   - **C** Professionalism
   - **D** Integrity *[1 mark]*

3 Which of the following is **not** part of the ethical framework in accounting?
   - **A** Aligning with business policy
   - **B** Complying with laws and regulations
   - **C** Ignoring professional standards
   - **D** Justifying one's actions *[1 mark]*

4 Which of the following refers to the accurate and unbiased reflection of the financial performance of a business?
   - **A** Objectivity
   - **B** Integrity
   - **C** Confidentiality
   - **D** Professional competence *[1 mark]*

5 Which of the following enhances the accuracy of financial reporting?
   - **A** Integrity
   - **B** Objectivity
   - **C** Professional competence
   - **D** All of the above *[1 mark]*

6 Which of the following is an example of a conflict of interest by an accountant?
   - **A** Applying for a job in a competing business
   - **B** Using client information for personal gain
   - **C** Meeting a business competitor for a personal reason
   - **D** Doing a part-time job after official hours *[1 mark]*

7 **a** State how strong ethical values:

   i) benefit the business stakeholders *[1 mark]*

   ....

   ii) positively impact society *[1 mark]*

   ....

   b Identify how the positive impacts of strong ethical values benefit a business. *[1 mark]*

   ....

8 **a** Define the principle of integrity. *[2 marks]*

   ....

26 Ethical considerations

b Explain how implementing the principle of integrity can affect investor trust. *[2 marks]*

....

....

....

9 Explain how applying an ethical framework in accounting helps to minimise:

   a operational risks *[2 marks]*

....

....

   b legal risks for businesses. *[2 marks]*

....

....

10 Ali is an accountant at a multinational company. He notices that a major customer has become insolvent but is still shown as trade receivable. The omission of irrecoverable debts or an allowance for irrecoverable debts has overstated both profit for the year and the asset of trade receivables. Ali's manager insists this is harmless and will help the company attract investors and meet its profit targets.

   a State the two ethical principles that are being compromised in this situation. *[2 marks]*

....

....

   b Suggest what Ali should do about this situation. *[2 marks]*

....

....

....

11 Hassan, an accountant, is unsatisfied with his current job as he has long working hours but a low salary. His supervisor often assigns him tasks outside his job description without any extra reward. A competitor of his current employer has offered Hassan a high-paying job. The competitor asks Hassan to bring confidential financial information from his current job as part of the deal.

Suggest how Hassan should respond. *[3 marks]*

....

....

....

....

7 ACCOUNTING CONCEPTS AND MODERN PRACTICES

12 Asma is a struggling sole trader and is desperate for someone to invest in her business. Yasmine is a potential investor, but Asma understands she must portray her financial statements positively if she wants Yasmine to agree to invest in her business. Asma has asked Samuel, a professional accountant, to show her assets at an artificially higher value in the financial statements to make them look more attractive to Yasmine. Asma has offered to pay a handsome fee to Samuel if he agrees.

Advise Samuel what the correct approach would be in this situation, outlining the principles that he should consider. Justify your answer. *[5 marks]*

13 a Explain what impact senior managers' behaviour can have on younger employees. *[2 marks]*

b Explain why it is important for senior managers to serve as role models by developing an ethical framework. *[2 marks]*

14 a Explain the concept of due care. *[2 marks]*

b Analyse the relationship between due care and the compilation of financial reports. *[2 marks]*

27 Technology and sustainability

1 A manual accounting system includes storing physical documents, which can lead to organisational problems. What is a challenge associated with this practice?

  A Enhanced document accessibility
  B Increased protection from unauthorised access
  C Scalability
  D Vulnerability to theft and damage *[1 mark]*

27 Technology and sustainability

2 Which of these benefits of data sustainability helps reduce the risk of regulatory penalties?
   A Improved environment
   B Increased confidence of stakeholders
   C Reduced risk of legal complications
   D Innovation *[1 mark]*

3 What is a potential consequence of a data breach?
   A Higher data storage costs
   B Damaged reputation
   C Increased data accuracy
   D Lower operational costs *[1 mark]*

4 Which of the following is **not** typically a feature of cloud storage services?
   A File backup service
   B Document management system
   C File-sharing services
   D Hardware failure recovery *[1 mark]*

5 Which strategy does **not** contribute to data security?
   A Allowing employees unrestricted access to sensitive data
   B Encrypting data against unauthorised access
   C Logging out of systems when not in use
   D Regularly updating antivirus software *[1 mark]*

6 What potential issue can arise from improperly deleting data from old hardware systems?
   A Increased energy consumption
   B Enhanced data security
   C Data leakage to unauthorised users
   D Reduced productivity *[1 mark]*

7 Why is having a disaster recovery plan for accounting data important?
   A To avoid regular audits
   B To ensure business continuity after data loss
   C To increase the risk of data breaches
   D To reduce the need for encryption *[1 mark]*

8 Explain why manual accounting might be unsuitable for a growing business. *[2 marks]*

   ....

   ....

   ....

9 Define encryption and describe its crucial role in digital accounting. *[2 marks]*

   ....

   ....

   ....

Photocopying prohibited   Cambridge IGCSE™ and O Level Accounting Workbook 2nd Edition

7 ACCOUNTING CONCEPTS AND MODERN PRACTICES

10 a State the difference between data safety and sustainability. *[2 marks]*

....

....

....

b Explain the importance of data safety and sustainability to an organisation. *[2 marks]*

....

....

....

c Describe how data sustainability practices can impact a business' environmental footprint. *[3 marks]*

....

....

....

....

11 Cloud storage has revolutionised the way businesses manage their accounting data.

a Discuss the role of cloud storage as a scalable solution for accounting data, especially as a business experiences growth. *[3 marks]*

....

....

....

b Suggest how cloud storage improves a business' disaster recovery capabilities, particularly after data loss incidents. *[3 marks]*

....

....

....

c Justify cloud storage as a more secure option for accounting data than storing data on local hard drives. *[3 marks]*

....

....

....

27 Technology and sustainability

12 a Discuss the potential impact of a data breach on a business' financial stability and overall reputation within the market. *[2 marks]*

....

....

....

b Discuss disruptions in business operations due to data loss and their effect on a company's financial performance. *[3 marks]*

....

....

....

....

Reinforce learning and deepen understanding of the key concepts covered in the latest Cambridge IGCSE™, IGCSE (9-1) and O Level Accounting syllabuses (0452/0985/7707) with this updated Workbook. An ideal course companion or homework book for use throughout the course.

» Develop and strengthen skills and knowledge with a wealth of additional exercises that perfectly supplement the updated Second Edition Student's Book.

» Build confidence with extra practice for each lesson to ensure that a topic is thoroughly understood before moving on.

» Consolidate knowledge of accounting procedures and principles of accounts with authentic exercises.

» Keep track of students' work with ready-to-go write-in exercises.

» Save time with all answers available FREE to download from: hachettelearning.com/answers-and-extras

This text has not been through the endorsement process for the Cambridge Pathway.

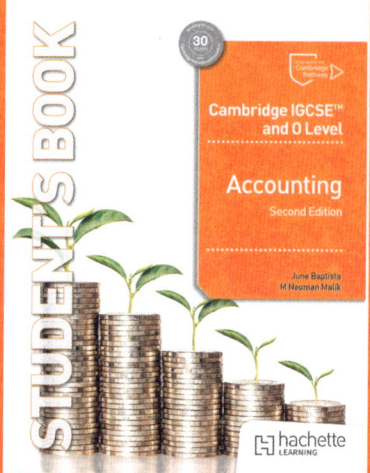

Also available:
Cambridge IGCSE and O Level Accounting Student's Book, Second Edition 9781036010621

The Student's Book is endorsed for the Cambridge Pathway.

For over 30 years we have been trusted by Cambridge schools around the world to provide quality support for teaching and learning.
For this reason we are an Endorsement Partner of Cambridge International Education and publish endorsed materials for their syllabuses.

Visit us at hachettelearning.com

ISBN 978-1-0360-1063-8